WAIT, That's Vegan?!

Plant-Based **Meatballs, Burgers, Steaks** and
Other Dishes **You Thought You'd Never Eat Again!**

Lisa Dawn Angerame, Creator of Lisa's Project: Vegan

PAGE STREET
PUBLISHING CO.

Copyright © 2020 Lisa Dawn Angerame

First published in 2020 by
Page Street Publishing Co.
27 Congress Street, Suite 105
Salem, MA 01970
www.pagestreetpublishing.com

Distributed by Macmillan, sales in Canada by The Canadian Manda Group.

24 23 22 21 20   1 2 3 4 5

ISBN-13: 978-1-62414-970-2
ISBN-10: 1-62414-970-7

Library of Congress Control Number: 2019941861

Cover and book design by Meg Baskis for Page Street Publishing Co.

Photography © Alex Shytsman
Printed and bound in China

For Paul and Luke

Contents

FOREWORD

We met Lisa over a decade ago, when she started frequenting Candle Cafe, our first restaurant on the Upper East Side in New York City. We always make it a point to get to know our patrons, and it wasn't long before we struck up a friendship. It was always a good day when we strolled through the restaurant and spotted Lisa sitting at the bar chatting with staff, or at a table with friends. Our conversations about food, veganism and health are something we continue to cherish to this day.

When we wrote our cookbook, *Vegan Holiday Cooking from Candle Cafe*, we asked Lisa if she would test recipes for us. In true Lisa spirit, she asked a lot of questions, gave us great suggestions and helped make our book the best it could be.

That experience showed us that our missions are completely aligned. What a pleasure and a true honor it has been to follow Lisa as she has documented her food journey on her blog, Lisa's Project: Vegan. We wholeheartedly share her passion for cooking tasty good food that happens to be vegan, and now she is sharing it for all to enjoy in this must-have cookbook.

Lisa makes it fun and delicious to cook with plants. Her innovative creations more than satisfy the palate as well as our nutritional needs. Lisa revitalizes old-time favorite recipes that wow even the most discerning eaters. There's no mystery here. The clarity and timing of this book fully embraces the evidence-based premise that a plant-based diet dramatically prevents and reverses many of the typical Western diseases including heart disease, certain cancers, diabetes, obesity and more. It also dramatically decreases one's carbon footprint, as well as the hazards of climate change.

Lisa provides recipes for food that is better tasting, better for you and better for the planet. Those who are fully committed to a vegan lifestyle, and even those who are not, will appreciate how important this book is.

Being in the kitchen with Lisa is natural and inviting. Just as with the Candle Restaurants' OG motto, "Food Fresh from Farm to Table," Lisa's delicious plant-based recipes are not only inspiring, they also raise the proverbial bar to new heights. With inventive recipes for Eggless Egg Salad (page 53), Carrot Lox (page 17), French toast (page 21), Meatless Meatballs (page 111), Beet Burgers (page 73), and of course, her famous Pecan Pie Squares (page 160), this book is sure to become a standout in your vegan cookbook collection.

You will enjoy making and eating these scrumptious vegan versions of all your favorites. As we have been saying at the Candle Restaurants for over 30 years, "All's Well that Eats Well," which is clearly evidenced in *Wait, That's Vegan?!*

In Food We Trust,

Joy Pierson & Bart Potenza
Founders of the Candle Restaurants

INTRODUCTION

So, you miss all of your favorite foods now that you are vegan? I get it. Once upon a time, I was there too—but those days are over! You don't have to feel nostalgic for your favorite foods anymore, because you now hold in your hands a book filled with them.

I became vegan over a decade ago after learning about how animals are raised for food, what animal agriculture does to the environment and how eating animals affects human health. I couldn't ignore the facts, and my mind was made up. The only problem was that I really didn't know what I was getting myself into.

There were so many things I had to give up—hello, all of my favorite foods—plus I only knew how to cook what my mother taught me to make. Eating at home was a big challenge so I just made a lot of pasta. Mainstream restaurants hardly had any obvious vegan or plant-based options besides roasted vegetables. And, at the time, there were only a handful of vegan restaurants in New York City. Luckily, I live only nine blocks away from my favorite one, Candle Cafe.

Even still, I wondered if I would be able to enjoy my old favorites ever again. Was it even possible to make vegan versions of them? Then I had a lightbulb moment. What if I took my old favorite recipes and figured out a way to make them vegan by leaving out unnecessary ingredients and using plant-based swaps instead? I love a good project, so I started experimenting with all kinds of combinations, permutations and replacements. I researched cooking techniques, food history and the "why" behind famous dishes. I took a plant-based cooking course and a plant-based nutrition course, and I started a blog to track it all called Lisa's Project: Vegan. Through the whole process, I realized two things: vegan cooking is no different than, well, cooking, and vegan food is just food that happens to be vegan.

Eventually, I figured out how to veganize my favorite dishes. And now you can too! Dive right into the breakfast chapter and whip up a frittata (page 25). You won't believe how close it is to the original flavors and texture. In the mood for an old-school sandwich? Skip the deli line and make a chickpea salad sandwich (page 64). It's so good you won't want to share it with anyone. Feeling ready to take on a main dish? There are so many nostalgic dishes in this book, pick one that you can't believe could be made vegan, such as the fettucine alfredo (page 71). That sauce is divine. Or if you love garlic, make the chickpea scampi immediately (page 90). Then go ahead and whip up a lasagna (page 127), call your friends and family over and wow them with a beautiful presentation. And of course, don't forget dessert. Brownies? Cookies? Whatever you make, people will be saying, "Are you sure this is vegan?"

In the end, that is why I wrote this book—to show that it only takes a few clever substitutions and all of your favorite foods can be made vegan.

So, what are you waiting for? Get cooking!

Lisa

BREAKFAST

and

BRUNCH

Let's start at the beginning, with breakfast, because it really is the most important meal of the day. Savory or sweet? Breakfast for one or brunch for a crowd? From pancakes and Benedicts to lox and frittatas, there is a recipe in this chapter for everyone.

Scrambled Tofu

Serves 2

Scrambled tofu is quintessential, the gateway meal for many new vegans. It is a great stand-in for scrambled eggs because tofu is so versatile; it can be mixed with any combination of vegetables, herbs and spices. This recipe calls for sautéed onions and peppers that are seasoned with Sazón, a savory blend of oregano, garlic, coriander, cumin and achiote. It brings a touch of heat and a beautiful color to this scramble. Finish it off with fresh parsley and lime juice, and serve it with avocado and tortillas.

Wait, you don't have time to sit down and eat? Wrap the scramble up in the tortillas for a breakfast burrito.

Scrambled Tofu

1 tbsp (15 ml) good olive oil

½ tsp turmeric

½ small onion, diced

¼ each yellow and orange pepper, diced

1 tbsp (12 g) Sazón

½ tsp chipotle powder

1 tbsp (16 g) tomato paste

2 tbsp (30 ml) water

7.5 oz (213 g) firm tofu, drained

2 tbsp (16 g) nutritional yeast

1 tsp kala namak

1 tbsp (15 ml) freshly squeezed lime juice

1 tbsp (4 g) chopped fresh parsley

To Serve

Flour tortillas

2 scallions, thinly sliced

1 avocado, peeled, pitted and sliced

Heat a skillet over medium heat. Add the oil. When it is shimmering, add the turmeric. Use a wooden spoon with a flat edge to stir the turmeric into the oil.

Add the onion and peppers, and mix to coat with the oil. Sauté until they are soft, 6 to 8 minutes. Add the Sazón and chipotle powder, and mix to coat the vegetables. Add the tomato paste and use the wooden spoon to mix it into the vegetables, cooking it for 3 to 4 minutes. Add the water. Simmer on low heat just until a light sauce forms, about 3 minutes.

Crumble the tofu into big pieces and add it to the skillet. Mix the tofu into the vegetables, breaking it up just a bit. Add the nutritional yeast and kala namak. Mix again and cook until the tofu is heated through, about 5 minutes. Add the lime juice and parsley, and mix one last time.

To warm the tortillas, preheat the oven to 350°F (175°C, or gas mark 4). Wrap the tortillas in foil, and place them in the oven for the last 10 minutes of the cooking time. Alternatively, you can warm them on a dry cast-iron skillet.

Portion out the scramble, and serve with tortillas, scallions and avocado.

NOTE:

Kala namak is also known as black salt, even though it is pink. It's a special salt that is mined in the Himalayas, and it's famous for its eggy, sulfuric flavor. It's an essential ingredient in this and several other recipes in this book. Don't skip it! It's what makes dishes like this work. You can find a bag in a South Asian market or online.

Carrot Lox

Serves 8

When I was growing up on Long Island, Sundays were for bagels. I loved going with my father to the bagel store in town to pick up a baker's dozen, a tub of cream cheese and a pound (454 g) of lox. When I became vegan, I had to figure out a way to replicate the main ingredient, lox, so I could still have Sundays with my dad. It took some work, but I finally came up with a formula to turn carrots into a soft, smoky, salty lox proxy.

4 large carrots, ends cut off and outer skin peeled

2 tsp (12 g) smoked salt

2 tsp (6 g) coconut sugar

½ cup (120 ml) aquafaba, room temperature

NOTE:

Aquafaba is the viscous liquid that results from cooking dried beans. It turns out that aquafaba is similar in its chemical makeup to eggs. Hence, the aquafaba craze started, and I've been experimenting with it ever since. All of the recipes in this book that call for aquafaba use the liquid from cooked chickpeas. A 15-ounce (425-g) can of chickpeas yields anywhere from ½ to ¾ cup (120 to 180 ml) of aquafaba. If you don't use it all for a recipe, store it in the refrigerator for up to 3 days or freezer for up to 3 months.

Make long slices of carrots, using a vegetable peeler, starting at one end of the carrot and peeling to the other. Turn the carrot after a few peels and peel again. Turn again and peel a few more peels. Turn and peel again. The carrot will start to look square, as if it has four sides. Keep peeling like this, going for long thick pieces. As you get closer to the core, the slices will get shorter. Stop peeling at that point.

Add the carrots to a container that has a cover. Sprinkle with the smoked salt and coconut sugar, and use a fork to mix it all together. Cover the container, and marinate the carrots in the refrigerator for 24 hours. After 12 hours, shake the container to redistribute the salt and sugar. After 24 hours, bring the carrots to room temperature. Place the marinated carrots in a strainer to drain any excess carrot juice.

Preheat the oven to 350°F (175°C, or gas mark 4). Place a piece of parchment paper on top of a piece of aluminum foil on a quarter sheet pan.

Add the aquafaba to a medium mixing bowl. Whisk it until it becomes foamy and white. Add the carrots and use a fork to mix them around. Be sure to coat all of the carrot slices.

Lift the carrots out of the bowl and pile them onto the middle of the parchment. Gently spread out the carrots with the fork, leaving a 1½-inch (3.5-cm) border. Pour any excess liquid over the carrots. Fold up the foil into a tight packet and bake for 25 minutes.

Remove the sheet pan from the oven and let the carrots steam in the packet for another 5 minutes. Open the packet and let the carrots stand until they cool completely.

Use right away or store in the refrigerator until ready to use. The lox will keep for up to 1 week, but I bet it won't last nearly that long!

Avocado Benedict
with Hollandaise Sauce

Makes 2

There are conflicting stories about the history of the famous eggs Benedict breakfast, but as an ex–Wall Street banker, my favorite one is about a broker named Lemuel Benedict. According to Wikipedia, he wandered into the Waldorf Hotel in 1894, hungover and hoping for a cure. He ordered buttered toast, poached eggs, crispy bacon and a hooker of hollandaise sauce. The maître d' was impressed with this combination and put it on the menu, subbing a toasted English muffin for the toast.

Like with many famous and familiar dishes, it is all about the sauce. In this vegan variation, the hollandaise plays a dual role, as both the sauce and the egg. It's super simple to whip up, and the flavor is out of this world. And, if you don't use all of the sauce for these Benedicts, save it for dinner and drizzle it over roasted vegetables, such as asparagus or broccoli.

Hollandaise Sauce

½ cup (120 ml) Cashew Cream (page 165)

1 tsp kala namak

1 tsp nutritional yeast

½ tsp freshly squeezed lemon juice

¼ tsp turmeric

Avocado Benedict

Vegan butter (page 166)

2 vegan English muffins, fork split, toasted

2 vine-ripened or heirloom tomatoes, sliced

1 avocado, peeled, pitted and sliced

Fresh pepper

To make the hollandaise sauce, add the cashew cream, kala namak, nutritional yeast, lemon juice and turmeric to a small bowl. Mix well. Use immediately, or store in a sealed container for up to 3 days in the refrigerator or up to 3 months in the freezer. If it has thickened up, add a splash of water and mix well.

To make the avocado Benedict, lightly butter the English muffins. Layer with slices of tomato and avocado. Pour the hollandaise sauce over the top and garnish with pepper.

French Bread French Toast

Makes 8

The minute I became vegan, I wanted French toast. But, how to veganize such a classic recipe without dredging the bread in eggs? A little vegan magic in the form of chickpea flour, also known as garbanzo bean flour or besan. When mixed with water, vanilla and a dash of cinnamon, it becomes the perfect new-fashioned way to make an old-fashioned dish.

I like to use baguettes for French toast because I think they have the perfect ratio of crust to crumb. Cut the bread into 1-inch (2.5-cm) slices. It's helpful to be close to exact: If sliced too thinly, the baguette pieces will become too soggy. If they're too thick, they won't be able to absorb enough batter. Not only that, but 1-inch (2.5-cm) slices are easily pierced with a fork and eaten in one or two bites.

French Toast

2 chickpea eggs (1 chickpea egg = 1 tbsp [6 g] chickpea flour + 3 tbsp [45 ml] water)

1 tsp vanilla extract

Dash or two of cinnamon

1 nutmeg, 5 scrapes on a microplane

Pinch of salt

8 (1-inch [2.5-cm]) baguette slices

Vegan butter (page 166), for cooking

To Serve

Maple syrup

Cinnamon

To make the French toast, start by making the chickpea eggs. In a bowl, whisk together the chickpea flour and water. Add the vanilla, cinnamon, nutmeg and salt. Whisk again to combine. Drop the baguette slices into the batter, flipping them over to coat both sides. Let the baguette slices soak for 2 minutes, flipping them once or twice.

Heat a cast-iron griddle or nonstick pan over medium heat, and add a dollop of butter. As it sizzles, use a spatula to coat the entire pan. Lift the baguette slices out of the batter, letting any excess drip off, and place them onto the griddle. Cook the first side for 2 or 3 minutes, until it starts to turn golden brown. Flip and cook the second side for 1 to 2 minutes. Depending on the size of the pan, this could take two or three rounds. Wipe out the pan in between each round and add new butter.

Serve with a drizzle of maple syrup and a dash of cinnamon.

Chocolate Chip Buttermilk Pancakes

Makes 8 to 12

I don't remember when I first learned how easy it is to make vegan buttermilk, but it's the key to amazing pancakes. Here's the deal: Apple cider vinegar acidulates nondairy milk to create a fermented version of itself, essentially a quick version of cultured dairy milk. From a food science point of view, it works the same way as buttermilk, tenderizing the gluten in the flour, yielding super light and fluffy pancakes. Stack them high on your plate and drizzle with chocolate maple syrup for a sweet breakfast treat.

Too much chocolate? Swap the chips for blueberries or sliced bananas.

Pancakes
1 cup (240 ml) unsweetened soy milk
1 tbsp (15 ml) apple cider vinegar
1 cup (125 g) all-purpose flour
2 tbsp (18 g) coconut sugar
1 tbsp (14 g) baking powder
¼ cup (60 g) vegan semisweet mini chocolate chips
Pinch of salt
Vegan butter (page 166)

Chocolate Maple Syrup
¼ cup (60 ml) dark maple syrup
2 tbsp (12 g) cocoa powder

To make the buttermilk, combine the milk and vinegar in a bowl, using a fork to whisk it together. Let stand for 5 minutes to acidulate. It will be lumpy.

To make the pancake batter, add the flour, coconut sugar and baking powder to a medium mixing bowl. Mix together. Pour the buttermilk into the flour mixture. Whisk until the batter is smooth and there are no lumps. Let the batter stand for 5 minutes; it will puff up a bit. Add the chocolate chips and salt, and mix well.

Heat a cast-iron griddle or nonstick pan over medium heat, and add a dollop of butter. As it sizzles, use a spatula to coat the entire pan. Scoop the batter into the pan, being sure not to crowd it, and cook until the tops start to bubble and look a little dry, about 5 minutes. Flip the pancakes over and cook for another minute. Remove the pancakes to a plate and set aside. Continue to make pancakes until all of the batter is gone, wiping out the pan and adding new butter in between batches.

To make the chocolate maple syrup, add the maple syrup and cocoa powder to a small bowl. Whisk until smooth. If you don't use it all, store it in a small jar in the cupboard, for up to a week.

To serve, stack the pancakes and drizzle with chocolate maple syrup.

Broccoli-Leek Frittata

Makes 8 slices

Frittatas are essentially omelets or crustless quiches. In this vegan version, the combination of all kinds of plant-based ingredients come together to create that familiar taste and texture. I have served this to vegans and carnivores alike, and it's an absolute crowd pleaser; there is never any left at the end of the party. It can be served warm, at room temperature or even cold, and it can be made up to two days in advance. Just cover in foil and reheat it for 30 minutes in a 350°F (175°C) oven.

Want to change it up? Try mushrooms and shallots, asparagus and onions, or tomatoes and corn.

Broccoli and Leeks

4 cups (364 g) chopped broccoli, leaves and stems removed and cut into bite-sized pieces

1 tbsp (15 ml) melted refined coconut oil

1 leek, white and light green parts, cleaned and cut into half-moons, about 1 cup (89 g)

2 cloves garlic, pressed

Pinch of salt

Custard

1 cup (240 ml) water

½ cup (73 g) cashews, soaked (see headnote, page 165)

7.5 oz (213 g) firm tofu, drained

1 (5.3-oz [150-g]) container plain unsweetened vegan yogurt

¼ cup (24 g) chickpea flour

¼ cup (60 ml) melted refined coconut oil

2 tbsp (16 g) nutritional yeast

1 tbsp (15 ml) tamari

1 tbsp (17 g) mellow white miso

½ tsp turmeric

Preheat the oven to 350°F (175°C, or gas mark 4). Set a 9¾-inch (25-cm) quiche dish on a half sheet pan.

To make the filling, add the broccoli florets to a pot and cover with water. Cover and bring the water to a boil. Cook until the florets turn bright green and are just al dente, about 5 minutes. Drain and add to a big mixing bowl.

Heat a cast-iron or nonstick skillet over low heat. Add the oil. When it is shimmering, add the leeks, garlic and salt, and use a wooden spoon to coat the vegetables. Cook until the leeks are bright and translucent, and the garlic is fragrant, 5 to 7 minutes.

Transfer the leeks and garlic into the bowl of broccoli. Mix to combine, and transfer to the quiche pan. Spread the mixture out evenly.

To make the custard, add the water, cashews, tofu, yogurt, chickpea flour, oil, nutritional yeast, tamari, miso and turmeric to a blender. Blend until combined and creamy, 1 to 2 minutes depending on your machine.

Pour the custard over the broccoli and leeks, distributing it evenly. Bake for at least 1 hour, or until the top has browned and the center is firm to the touch.

As it cools, the top will deflate just a bit and the quiche will continue to firm up. Slice and serve.

Chia Seed Pudding Neapolitans

Serves 4

Chia seed pudding is a great vegan staple to have on hand because these little seeds are nutrition powerhouses, packed with omega-3s, fiber, protein, antioxidants, calcium and magnesium. When soaked, they puff up and take on an almost tapioca pudding–like texture.

I like to serve these as Neapolitans, as a fun take on the famous vanilla-chocolate-strawberry ice cream combination. The vanilla pudding layer is enhanced by specks of ground vanilla beans, which have an intense vanilla flavor, and reminds me of old-fashioned vanilla ice cream. The chocolate pudding layer is made with raw cacao powder, and the strawberry layer is just fresh strawberries. Make these little jars of goodness the night before and grab one for an on-the-go breakfast or mid-morning power snack.

Vanilla Chia Seed Pudding

¾ cup (180 ml) cashew milk (page 174)

2 tbsp (30 ml) golden maple syrup

2 tbsp (20 g) white chia seeds

¼ tsp ground vanilla beans

Chocolate Chia Seed Pudding

¾ cup (180 ml) cashew milk (page 174)

2 tbsp (30 ml) dark maple syrup

2 tbsp (20 g) white chia seeds

1 tbsp (6 g) raw cacao powder

Neapolitans

6 big strawberries, hulled and sliced

To make the vanilla chia seed pudding, add the cashew milk, maple syrup, chia seeds and vanilla beans to a small container with a lid. Cover and shake well, ensuring that there are no clumps of chia seeds. Refrigerate for at least 2 hours or overnight.

To make the chocolate chia seed pudding, add the cashew milk, maple syrup, chia seeds and raw cacao powder to a separate small container with a lid. Use a fork to whisk the cacao into the milk. Then cover the container and shake well, ensuring that there are no clumps of cacao powder or chia seeds. Refrigerate for at least 2 hours or overnight.

To assemble the Neapolitans, divide the chocolate pudding amongst four jars or small bowls. Divide the strawberries and layer them on top of the chocolate pudding. Divide the vanilla pudding and layer it on top of the strawberries. Serve immediately or store in a sealed container in the refrigerator for up to 5 days.

Sweet Fruit-Filled Crepes

with Cinnamon Cream

Makes 6

Crepes sound elegant, but they are actually street food in France. I remember my first trip to Paris, seeing creperies all over the city, and marveling at how Parisians can make fast food seem fancy! Vegan crepes are so easy to make you won't believe it. They don't require a special crepe pan either, just a good old-fashioned cast-iron griddle pan or nonstick skillet. Once you get the technique down, you are going to want to invite everyone over for Sunday brunch to impress them with your crepe-making skills.

Cinnamon Cream
¼ cup (60 ml) Cashew Cream (page 165)
1 tbsp (15 ml) golden maple syrup
1 tsp vanilla extract
⅛ tsp cinnamon
Pinch of salt

Crepes
½ cup (46 g) chickpea flour
2 tbsp (16 g) arrowroot starch/flour
2 tbsp (18 g) coconut sugar
1 cup (240 ml) unsweetened soy milk
1 tsp vanilla extract
Pinch of salt
Vegan butter (page 166), for cooking

To Serve
Sliced bananas
Sliced strawberries
Blueberries

To make the cinnamon cream, mix the cashew cream, maple syrup, vanilla, cinnamon and salt together.

To make the crepes, add the chickpea flour, arrowroot and coconut sugar to a medium mixing bowl. Whisk to combine. Add the milk, vanilla and salt. Whisk together until completely smooth.

Heat a cast-iron griddle or nonstick pan over medium heat and add a dollop of butter. As it sizzles, use a spatula to coat the entire pan. Scoop up a scant ¼-cup (60-ml) measure of batter and pour it onto the pan. Quickly pick up the pan, tip it gently and rotate it around to distribute the crepe batter in a thin circle. Return to the heat and cook until the edges start to brown and the top looks dry. Carefully flip the crepe over and cook the other side for another minute. When the first crepe is done, gently place it on a big plate. Cook the remaining crepes and pile them on the plate, covering them with a towel, until all the batter is gone.

To assemble the crepes, layer bananas and strawberries on one half of each crepe. Fold it in half and then in half again, like a little triangle package. Top with blueberries and a drizzle of cinnamon cream.

Mini Banana Bread Loaves

Makes 2

Banana bread is the ultimate quick bread. It's really easy to make vegan by using ground flax to replace eggs. I love making these little loaves with coconut sugar, which has a warm, caramel flavor. I serve them for breakfast or even as an after-school snack.

¼ cup (60 ml) melted refined coconut oil, plus extra for brushing

1 flax egg (1 flax egg = 1 tbsp [7 g] flax meal + 3 tbsp [45 ml] water)

3 ripe big bananas

2 tsp (10 ml) freshly squeezed lemon juice

1 cup (144 g) coconut sugar

1 tsp vanilla extract

1½ cups (188 g) all-purpose flour

1 tsp baking soda

½ tsp salt

Preheat the oven to 350°F (175°C, or gas mark 4). Lightly brush two mini loaf pan wells with oil.

To make the flax egg, use a fork to whisk together the flax and water. Set aside for 5 minutes to thicken.

Add the bananas and lemon juice to a medium mixing bowl. Use the back of a fork to mash the bananas into the lemon juice really well. It's okay if there are still a few lumps. Add the flax egg, coconut sugar, ¼ cup (60 ml) of oil and vanilla. Mix well.

In a separate big mixing bowl, add the flour, baking soda and salt. Mix together well. Pour the banana mixture into the flour mixture. Mix until a batter forms and the flour is fully incorporated.

Split the batter evenly into the two mini loaf pans. Bake for 30 to 35 minutes, until the tops are firm and a tester comes out clean.

Let the loaves cool a bit, remove them from the pans and place them onto a cooling rack to cool completely. Slice and serve.

VARIATIONS

This batter can also be used to make a big loaf, standard muffins or mini muffins. Here are the approximate yields and baking times:

1 big loaf, 55 to 60 minutes

12 standard muffins, 25 to 30 minutes

30 mini muffins, 12 to 15 minutes

Meyer Lemon Ricotta Pancakes

Makes 8 to 12

There is something elegant about the combination of fresh lemon juice and ricotta. In these grown-up pancakes, Meyer lemons are the star of the show. A cross between a lemon and a Mandarin orange, they are acidic like lemons, but their juice is a touch sweet like oranges. The addition of fresh ricotta yields a pancake with a creamy center that is kind of irresistible. So, leave the chocolate chips for the kids, make these sexy pancakes for your adult brunch and serve them with your favorite brunch cocktail!

Pancakes

1 cup (240 ml) unsweetened soy milk

1 tbsp (15 ml) freshly squeezed Meyer lemon juice

1 cup (125 g) all-purpose flour

2 tbsp (18 g) coconut sugar

1 tbsp (14 g) baking powder

2 tbsp (12 g) Meyer lemon zest

¼ cup (57 g) Almond Ricotta (page 169)

1 tsp vanilla extract

Pinch of salt

Vegan butter (page 166), for cooking

To Serve

1 Meyer lemon, thinly sliced

Fresh blueberries

Maple syrup

To make the buttermilk, combine the milk and lemon juice, using a fork to whisk them together. Let it stand for 5 minutes to acidulate. It will be lumpy.

To make the pancake batter, add the flour, coconut sugar and baking powder to a medium mixing bowl. Mix together. Pour the buttermilk into the flour mixture. Mix together until the batter is smooth and there are no lumps. Let the batter stand for 5 minutes; it will puff up a bit. Add the lemon zest, ricotta, vanilla and salt, and mix well.

Heat a cast-iron griddle or nonstick pan over medium heat, and add a dollop of butter. As it sizzles, use a spatula to coat the entire pan. Scoop the batter onto the pan, being sure not to crowd it, and cook until the tops start to bubble and look a little dry. Flip the pancakes over and cook for another minute. Remove the pancakes to a plate and set aside. Continue to make pancakes until all of the batter is gone, wiping out the pan and adding new butter in between batches.

To serve, caramelize the lemons. Heat a separate small cast-iron or nonstick pan over medium heat. Add the lemon slices and cook for 3 minutes without moving the lemons until the first side is brown and soft. Use tongs to gently flip the slices over. Cook for another 2 minutes.

Arrange the pancakes on a plate along with the caramelized lemon slices and blueberries. Drizzle with maple syrup.

NOTE:

Use a microplane or citrus zester to zest your lemons, limes and oranges before squeezing them. Be careful to stop when you get to the white pith, which tends to be bitter.

Chickpea Shakshouka

with Avocados and Fresh Herbs

Serves 2

Shakshouka is a dish that has roots both in the Middle East and North Africa, and it is a fun dish to veganize. The traditional preparation calls for eggs to be poached over tomato broth spiced up with coriander, paprika and other flavors. But who needs the eggs? Not us! Instead, in this variation, chickpeas are added right into the sauce, along with extra vegetables, Aleppo pepper and a hit of nutmeg for a flavorful, hearty, protein-packed situation. You don't have to wait for breakfast to eat it, either. It is a great busy weeknight meal; serve it right out of the skillet with a side of crusty bread to sop up all that delicious sauce.

Shakshouka

1 tbsp (15 ml) good olive oil

½ small onion, diced

2 cloves garlic, pressed

1 yellow bell pepper, diced

1 small zucchini, diced

1 tsp Aleppo pepper

½ tsp coriander

½ tsp paprika

1 nutmeg, 10 scrapes on a microplane

Pinch of salt and a dash of pepper

¼ cup (66 g) tomato paste

1 cup (240 ml) water

1½ cups (300 g) cooked or 1 (15-oz [425-g]) can chickpeas, drained

To Serve

1 avocado, split in half, pitted, peeled and sliced

1 tbsp (4 g) chopped fresh parsley

1 tbsp (6 g) chopped fresh mint

Crusty bread

Heat the oil in a cast-iron or nonstick skillet over medium heat. When it is shimmering, add the onion and sauté until translucent, about 3 to 4 minutes. Add the garlic, yellow pepper, zucchini, Aleppo pepper, coriander, paprika, nutmeg, salt and pepper. Cook until the vegetables are soft, about 8 minutes.

Add the tomato paste. Use a wooden spoon to mix it into the vegetables, cooking it for 3 to 4 minutes.

Add the water and the chickpeas, and mix to form a sauce. Simmer until the sauce has reduced and thickened, about 20 minutes.

Take the pan off the heat. Place the avocado slices on top of the chickpea mixture, and sprinkle with parsley and mint. Serve in the skillet with crusty bread on the side.

NOTE:

Parsley is more than just a garnish, it's a really healthy green that is high in vitamins A, K and C, and it's also a rich source of antioxidants. Keep a bouquet of parsley in fresh water on the counter or refrigerator and snip some off when a recipe calls for it.

SALADS

and

SANDWICHES

Famous salads and sandwiches are transformed using all kinds of plant-based ingredients. From egg salad and carpaccio to Caesar salad and eggplant Parmesan, by the time you've eaten everything in this chapter, you will never want the originals again.

Corned Tempeh Reubens on Rye

Makes 2

The first time I had a tempeh Reuben was at Angelica Kitchen in New York City. That first bite brought me back to all the times I ate Reuben sandwiches at the deli with my family. It was kind of a revelation; the moment I realized that if I worked hard enough on a recipe for a dish I used to eat, I could make a delicious vegan version. This Reuben is an ode to those old days, with just a few plant-based substitutions.

The tempeh is marinated and cooked in a variety of spices reminiscent of the flavors of corned beef. Give yourself a little time to prep this and you too will be transported right back to your pre-vegan days.

Corned Tempeh

1 (8-oz [226-g]) package tempeh, cut into 8 square pieces
2 tbsp (30 ml) tamari
2 bay leaves
2 tsp (2 g) coriander seeds
2 tsp (2 g) juniper berries
2 tsp (2 g) allspice berries
2 tsp (3 g) peppercorns
2 tsp (7 g) mustard seeds
2-inch (5-cm) piece of peeled ginger, cut into a few chunks
3 cups (720 ml) water

Thousand Island Dressing

¼ cup (60 ml) vegan mayo
¼ cup (60 ml) ketchup
3 tbsp (45 g) diced pickles
1 tsp apple cider vinegar
1 tsp coconut sugar

Reubens

4 pieces rye bread, toasted
Sauerkraut

To make the tempeh, place the tempeh squares in a pot. Add the tamari, bay leaves, coriander seeds, juniper berries, allspice berries, peppercorns, mustard seeds and ginger. Cover with the water and bring to a boil. Reduce to a simmer and cook, uncovered, for 30 to 45 minutes, until the liquid reduces by half but still covers the tempeh.

Preheat the oven to 350°F (175°C, or gas mark 4). Line a half sheet pan with parchment paper. Using tongs, lift the tempeh out of the pot, place it on the sheet pan and bake for 30 minutes, until the tempeh is nice and brown. Use it immediately, or store it in a sealed container for up to 1 week in the refrigerator.

To make the Thousand Island dressing, mix the mayo, ketchup, pickles, vinegar and coconut sugar together. Serve immediately or store in the refrigerator in a sealed jar for up to 1 week.

To assemble the Reubens, spread the Thousand Island dressing on the rye toast. Layer with tempeh and sauerkraut. Top with the other piece of toast and serve.

Salt-Cured Beet Carpaccio

Serves 8

Beets are one of my all-time favorite vegetables. They come in lots of pretty colors, and they are earthy, sweet and sometimes a little bitter. A perfect flavor combination, all in one vegetable! I love experimenting with them to see what I can turn them into.

In this preparation, they are transformed into a whole new version of themselves: The beets are thinly sliced and marinated overnight in salt. Then they're steam roasted, just like their carrot cousins for Carrot Lox (page 17). They become silky soft and melt-in-your-mouth delicious, a fun facsimile of beef carpaccio. Served with a creamy roasted garlic dressing, fresh basil and capers, this platter will wow anyone who sits at your table.

Beet Carpaccio

2 large red or candy cane beets, peeled and thinly sliced on a mandoline

2 tsp (12 g) sea salt

½ cup (120 ml) aquafaba, room temperature

To make the carpaccio, add the beets to a container that has a cover. Sprinkle with sea salt and use a fork to mix it all together. Cover the container, and marinate the beets in the refrigerator for 24 hours.

After 12 hours, shake the container to redistribute the salt. After 24 hours, bring the beets to room temperature. Add the marinated beets to a strainer to drain any excess beet juice.

Preheat the oven to 350°F (175°C, or gas mark 4). Place a piece of parchment paper on top of a piece of aluminum foil on a quarter sheet pan.

Add the aquafaba to a medium mixing bowl. Whisk it until it becomes foamy and white. Add the beets and use a fork to mix them around. Be sure to coat all of the beets.

Lift the beets out of the bowl and pile them onto the middle of the parchment. Gently spread out the beets with the fork, leaving a 1½-inch (3.5-cm) border. Pour any excess liquid over the beets. Fold up into a tight packet and bake for 25 minutes.

Remove the sheet pan from the oven and let the beets steam in the packet for another 5 minutes. Open the packet and let the beets stand until they cool completely.

Use right away or store in the refrigerator until ready to use. The beets will keep for up to 1 week.

(Continued)

Creamy Roasted Garlic Dressing

½ cup (120 ml) Cashew Cream (page 165)

2 tbsp (30 ml) good olive oil

2 tbsp (30 ml) freshly squeezed lemon juice

2 tsp (10 g) roasted garlic

2 tsp (11 g) mellow white miso

1 tsp sherry vinegar

1 tsp Grainy Mustard (page 170)

¼ tsp coconut sugar

Pinch of salt

To Serve

A few leaves of basil, cut into chiffonade

A few spoonfuls of capers

Fresh pepper

1 Macadamia nut, a few scrapes on a microplane

To make the dressing, add the cashew cream, oil, lemon juice, garlic, miso, vinegar, mustard, coconut sugar and salt to a blender. Blend until smooth. Use immediately, or store in a sealed container in the refrigerator for up to 1 week or in the freezer for up to 3 months. If it has thickened up, add a splash of water and mix well.

To assemble the carpaccio, spoon a bit of dressing on a serving platter. Arrange the beets on top of the dressing. Drizzle with a little more dressing, and decorate with basil and capers. Top with pepper and shaved macadamia.

NOTE:

To roast garlic, preheat the oven to 350°F (175°C, or gas mark 4). Place a piece of parchment paper on top of a piece of aluminum foil on a quarter sheet pan. Peel the outer layer of paper off the garlic bulb and cut just the very top off to expose the cloves. Place the garlic on the parchment paper and drizzle with a little olive oil. Wrap it up tightly and bake for 45 minutes, until the garlic cloves are brown and caramelized. When the garlic has cooled to the touch, squeeze out the cloves and mash with a fork. Use immediately, or store in a sealed container in the refrigerator for up to 3 days or in the freezer for 3 months.

Eggplant Parmesan Hero

Makes 4

I've been making eggplant Parmesan heroes since high school because they are my dad's favorite. He and I spent a lot of time tinkering with the best way to prep the eggplant, specifically for sandwiches. We came up with a method that results in the most excellent eggplant Parmesan heroes. As with other vegetarian dishes, the main swap here is the cheese. Cashews come to the rescue in the form of melty, creamy, cheesy goodness that makes these heroes just as good as any you would find at your local Italian place.

Eggplant

1 big eggplant, sliced into about 24 thin rounds

A few big pinches of salt

2 chickpea eggs (1 chickpea egg = 1 tbsp [6 g] chickpea flour + 3 tbsp [45 ml] water)

Dash of pepper

½ cup (64 g) Seasoned Breadcrumbs (page 178)

Olive oil, for frying

Line a half sheet pan with paper towels. Place as many eggplant rounds as you can fit in one layer on the paper towels. Sprinkle with salt. Lay a paper towel on top of the eggplants and add another layer of eggplant rounds. Sprinkle with salt and cover with another layer of paper towels. Top the whole thing with another half sheet pan, and weigh it down with a couple of heavy pots. Let stand for at least 30 minutes.

To make the chickpea eggs, whisk the chickpea flour and water together. Pour them into a shallow bowl or breading dish. Season with salt and pepper.

Pour the breadcrumbs into a separate shallow bowl or breading dish.

Have two big plates at the ready, one for the breaded eggplants and one with a paper towel on it for the fried eggplants.

Dredge the eggplant in the chickpea eggs, coating both sides well, letting any excess drip off. Dredge the eggplant through the breadcrumbs, pressing the eggplant round into the breadcrumbs to make sure the breadcrumbs stick. Set them on the first plate.

Heat the oil in a cast-iron pan or nonstick skillet over medium heat. When the oil is shimmering, gently lay a few eggplants onto the oil. Fry until the eggplants start to look translucent on the top side, about 5 minutes. Carefully flip them over to cook the second side for another three minutes. The eggplant rounds should be translucent and the breadcrumbs dark and crispy. Lay the cooked eggplant on the paper towel–lined plate. Finish cooking the rest of the eggplants.

(Continued)

Eggplant Parmesan Hero (Continued)

4 hero rolls, split

All-Purpose Red Sauce (page 173)

1 cup (240 ml) cashew milk (page 174)

2 tsp (6 g) arrowroot starch/flour

2 tsp (6 g) nutritional yeast

¼ tsp garlic powder

¼ tsp onion powder

⅛ tsp mustard powder

Pinch of salt

Almond Parmesan (page 177)

To make the heroes, preheat the oven to 350°F (175°C, or gas mark 4). Line a half sheet pan with parchment paper.

Place the hero rolls on the baking tray and toast in the oven, about 10 minutes.

In the meantime, heat the sauce and make the melty cheese. Add the sauce to a small saucepan and heat it through, about 5 minutes. To make the melty cheese, add the cashew milk, arrowroot, nutritional yeast, garlic powder, onion powder, mustard powder and salt to a small pot. Bring to a low simmer, constantly whisking the mixture until it thickens up and starts to pull away from the sides of the pot and stick to the whisk, about 2 minutes.

To assemble the heroes, ladle some sauce on the bottom side of the toasted rolls. Layer with eggplant slices, overlapping them slightly, and a drizzle of melty cashew cheese sauce. Sprinkle with Parmesan and cover with the top of the hero roll. Serve immediately.

Chinese Tofu Salad

Serves 2

I didn't come across Chinese chicken salad until I went to college in Los Angeles. I am glad I did because it has great texture—crunch from two kinds of cabbage, lots of carrots, scallions and cucumbers—and great flavor. With well-seasoned tofu subbing for the chicken, and Mandarin oranges and toasted almonds adding texture and flavor, it's a salad that will fast become part of your regular rotation.

Tofu

1 tbsp (15 ml) sunflower oil
1 tbsp (15 ml) tamari
½ tsp garlic powder
½ tsp ground ginger
Pinch of salt and a dash of pepper
7.5 oz (213 g) extra firm tofu, pressed for 10 minutes and cut into strips

Toasted Almonds

½ cup (72 g) blanched almonds

Sesame Vinaigrette

1 clove garlic
1 tsp grated ginger
3 tbsp (45 ml) apple cider vinegar
1 tbsp (15 ml) Mandarin orange juice, from a can of Mandarin oranges
¼ cup (60 ml) sesame oil
1 tbsp (15 ml) tamari
1 tsp mirin
1 tsp dark maple syrup

Salad

2 cups (140 g) shredded Napa cabbage
1 cup (70 g) shredded purple cabbage
1 cup (110 g) shredded carrot
4 scallions, white and green parts, thinly sliced
2 Kirby cucumbers, thinly sliced
1 (10-oz [283-g]) can mandarin oranges

To make the tofu, preheat the oven to 350°F (175°C, or gas mark 4). Line a half sheet pan with parchment paper.

Add the oil, tamari, garlic powder and ginger to a medium mixing bowl. Whisk together and season with a little salt and pepper. Add the tofu to the bowl and toss to coat the tofu well. Arrange the tofu in a single layer on the sheet pan and bake for 30 minutes.

At the halfway mark for the tofu, toast the almonds. Line a quarter sheet pan with parchment paper. Arrange the almonds in a single layer. Bake for 10 to 15 minutes, until the almonds have turned a few shades darker. Cool and coarsely chop.

In the meantime, to make the vinaigrette, add the garlic and ginger to a glass jar with a lid or to a dressing bottle. Cover with the vinegar and Mandarin orange juice, and let sit for 15 minutes to macerate. Add the oil, tamari, mirin and maple syrup. Cover the container and shake well to combine. The dressing will separate, so shake well before using.

To assemble the salad, add the cabbages, carrot, scallions and cucumbers to a big salad bowl. Pour the dressing over the top and toss to combine. Top with mandarin oranges, baked tofu and toasted almonds. Serve immediately.

Wait, That's Vegan?!

Crispy Tempeh Bacon BLTs
with Herbed Mayo

Makes 4

The BLT is one of the most famous sandwiches ever invented and one of the first things new vegans crave. With just three ingredients—smoky bacon, crunchy lettuce and juicy tomatoes—it needs nothing more than some good toasted bread and a little herbed up mayo. It's pretty effortless to veganize, with tempeh standing in for the bacon. Baked to a crisp in a smoky, sticky marinade, the tempeh can be made in advance and stored in a sealed container in the refrigerator for up to a week—if it lasts that long! When you are ready to make your BLTs, take the bacon out and let it sit on the counter until it comes to room temperature.

Tempeh Bacon

1 (8-oz [226-g]) package soy tempeh, thinly sliced the short way, about 24 pieces

2 tbsp (30 ml) dark maple syrup

2 tbsp (30 ml) tamari

2 tbsp (30 ml) balsamic vinegar

2 tbsp (30 ml) sunflower oil

2 tbsp (16 g) nutritional yeast

2 tbsp (18 g) coconut sugar

2 tsp (12 g) smoked salt

Herbed Mayo

¼ cup (60 ml) vegan mayo

1 tsp chopped fresh basil

1 tsp chopped fresh parsley

1 tsp chopped fresh chives

BLTs

8 pieces of your favorite bread, toasted

4 pieces of lettuce

4 small vine-ripened tomatoes, sliced

To prep the tempeh, place the sliced tempeh in a saucepan and cover with water. Bring to a boil. Reduce the heat and simmer, uncovered, for 10 minutes.

Preheat the oven to 350°F (175°C, or gas mark 4).

To make the tempeh bacon marinade, add the maple syrup, tamari, balsamic vinegar, oil, nutritional yeast, coconut sugar and smoked salt to a small bowl. Whisk together. Pour the marinade into a baking dish that is wide enough to hold all of the tempeh in one layer.

When the tempeh has finished simmering, lift it out of the water with tongs. Gently lay each piece into the marinade, flipping it over to coat both sides.

Bake the tempeh for 40 to 45 minutes, or until the marinade is mostly absorbed, and the tempeh is crispy around the edges. Remove from the oven, lift the tempeh out of the baking dish with tongs and place it on a plate to cool completely.

To make the herbed mayo, mix the mayo, basil, parsley and chives together well. Use immediately, or store in a sealed container in the refrigerator for up to 1 week.

To assemble the BLTs, spread the herbed mayo on the toast. Layer with tempeh bacon, lettuce and tomatoes. Top with another piece of toast. Slice and serve.

Greek Salad

with Orzo and Almond Feta

Serves 4

This Greek salad is the epitome of the casual meal. In this version, orzo, Kalamata olives and almond feta are tossed with red wine vinaigrette. The flavor pairings are timeless, and it's a great salad to serve at a barbecue or a pool party.

Almond Feta

1 cup (143 g) blanched almonds, soaked overnight, drained and rinsed

¼ cup (60 ml) water

2 tbsp (30 ml) good olive oil

2 tbsp (30 ml) freshly squeezed lemon juice

2 tsp (10 ml) ume plum vinegar

¼ tsp salt

Red Wine Vinaigrette

1 clove garlic, pressed

2 tbsp (30 ml) red wine vinegar

2 tbsp (30 ml) freshly squeezed lemon juice

¼ cup (60 ml) good olive oil

¼ tsp dried oregano

¼ tsp salt

Orzo

1 cup (168 g) uncooked orzo

Salad

4 mini cucumbers, peeled and cut into half-moons

8 small vine-ripened tomatoes, cut into quarters

1 cup (160 g) diced red onion

4 scallions, thinly sliced

½ cup (90 g) pitted Kalamata olives, coarsely chopped

¼ cup (16 g) chopped fresh dill

2 tbsp (8 g) chopped fresh parsley

To make the almond feta, add the almonds into the food processor along with the water, oil, lemon juice, vinegar and salt. Process, stopping to scrape down the sides often, until the mixture is smooth and creamy. This could take up to 5 minutes. Spoon the almond mixture into a nut milk bag or double-lined cheesecloth. Twist it and tie it tightly. Place it on a fine-mesh strainer over a bowl, cover and let it stand on the counter overnight.

Preheat the oven to 300°F (150°C, or gas mark 2). Line a quarter sheet pan with parchment paper. Remove the almond cheese from the nut milk bag or cheesecloth; it will be compact and easy to work with. Form it into a flat disk, about 1-inch (2.5-cm) thick, place it on the sheet pan and bake for 20 to 25 minutes, until just firm. Remove the pan from the oven and set aside.

To make the red wine vinaigrette, add the garlic to a glass jar with a lid or to a dressing bottle. Cover with the vinegar and lemon juice and let sit for 15 minutes to macerate. Add the oil, oregano and salt. Cover the container and shake well to combine. The dressing will separate, so shake well before using.

To make the orzo, bring a large pot of salted water to a boil. Cook the orzo according to the package instructions. Drain, place it into a big mixing bowl and immediately toss with the vinaigrette. Add the cucumbers, tomatoes, onion, scallions, olives, dill and parsley. Crumble the almond feta over the salad and mix gently to combine. Serve warm or at room temperature.

Eggless Egg Salad

Makes 2 cups (about 500 g)

Egg salad was one my favorite lunch foods growing up. Whenever my parents came to visiting day at camp, I always requested that my father make his famous version, which I would pile on raisin pumpernickel bread. I loved it for a few reasons—the crispy celery, the velvety mashed-up eggs and the secret splooshes of ketchup for just the right mix of sweet, savory, creamy and crunchy. Every time I make this now, I am reminded of those summers sitting by the lake enjoying lunch with my family.

In this version, beans sub for the eggs. I tested all the different white beans—navy, butter, cannellini and white kidney beans—and the clear winner is navy. To make it eggy, I add kala namak, and for that familiar yellow color, I add turmeric powder. You will be pleasantly surprised at the color, texture and taste of this vegan version. Eat it on top of a salad or on your favorite bread. For me, that's still raisin pumpernickel!

1½ cups (300 g) cooked or 1 (15-oz [425-g]) can navy beans, drained, divided

½ tsp turmeric

½ tsp kala namak

½ cup (51 g) diced celery

2 tbsp (6 g) thinly sliced chives

¼ cup (60 ml) vegan mayo

1 tbsp (15 ml) ketchup

½ tsp ume plum vinegar

Measure out ¼ cup (71 g) of beans and set aside. Add the remaining beans to the food processor and pulse a few times to break them down.

Turn out the processed beans into a big mixing bowl. Add the turmeric, kala namak, celery, chives, mayo, ketchup and vinegar. Mix together gently to incorporate everything. Add the reserved beans and mix to combine.

Serve immediately, or store in the refrigerator in a sealed container for up to 5 days.

Salad Niçoise

Serves 4 to 6

My mother took me on a trip to the south of France for my thirtieth birthday, and together, we ate our weight in Salad Niçoise and baguettes. We loved how each restaurant served a slightly different version of the salad. When we came home, I decided it would be fun to make our own version that took the best elements from each. I tweaked it after going vegan by subbing flavorful tempeh for the tuna and creating a savory dressing with miso and mustard. Now, when I make it for us to share, we always chuckle because there's a lot of controversy in Nice about what makes a Salad Niçoise a Salad Niçoise. Who knows what they would say about this version, but we say, "très délicieux!"

Miso Mustard Dressing

¼ cup (60 ml) freshly squeezed lemon juice

1 clove garlic

2 tbsp (34 g) mellow white miso

1 tbsp (15 ml) Grainy Mustard (page 170)

1 tsp golden maple syrup

¼ cup (60 ml) good olive oil

Pinch of salt

Tempeh

1 (8-oz [226-g]) package soy tempeh, cut into small cubes

¼ cup (60 ml) tamari

¼ cup (32 g) nutritional yeast

2 tbsp (30 ml) sunflower oil

To make the miso mustard dressing, add the lemon juice and garlic to a small mixing bowl. Stir it around and let it sit for 15 minutes to macerate. Add the miso, mustard, maple syrup, oil and salt. Use a whisk to break up the miso and then whisk everything together until the dressing is completely smooth. Store in a glass jar with a lid or a dressing bottle.

To make the tempeh, place the cubed tempeh in a saucepan and cover with water. Bring to a boil. Reduce the heat and simmer, uncovered, for 10 minutes.

In a medium mixing bowl, whisk together the tamari and nutritional yeast. Lift the tempeh out of the water with tongs and add it to the marinade. Toss to cover all of the tempeh and marinate it for 10 minutes.

Heat the oil in a cast-iron or nonstick skillet. When it is shimmering, add the tempeh and cook over medium heat, moving it around with tongs to try to get all sides crispy, about 8 minutes. Take the pan off the heat and let stand until the rest of the salad is ready.

(Continued)

Salad Niçoise (Continued)

Salad

1 cup (110 g) haricot vert or green beans, ends trimmed

1 cup (149 g) mixed cherry or grape tomatoes, halved

1 tbsp (15 ml) good olive oil

Pinch of salt

1 red bell pepper, cut into matchsticks

1 (14-oz [397-g]) can artichoke hearts, drained, cut in half

½ cup (90 g) Niçoise olives

½ cup (90 g) pitted green olives

2 Kirby cucumbers, thinly sliced on a mandoline

2 big radishes, thinly sliced on a mandoline

2 tsp (1 g) chopped fresh parsley

2 tsp (3 g) chopped fresh dill

2 tsp (2 g) chopped fresh chives

To prepare the haricot vert or green beans, fill a big bowl with ice cubes and cold water. Bring a pot of water to boil. Using a spider strainer, gently drop the haricot vert into the boiling water and cook for 3 minutes. Lift them out with the spider strainer and drop them right into the ice bath for 1 minute. Lay them out onto a kitchen towel to dry.

To prepare the tomatoes, toss them with the oil and a pinch of salt. Set aside.

To assemble the salad, arrange the tempeh, haricot vert, tomatoes, bell pepper, artichoke hearts, olives, cucumbers and radishes on a big platter in a pleasing way. Sprinkle with parsley, dill and chives. Serve with the dressing on the side.

Cobb Salad

Serves 2

Cobb salad is a staple on menus everywhere. What sets it apart is the presentation—a bed of lettuce topped with rows of all kinds of deliciousness. In this nod to the original, three different lettuces are tossed with a lemon shallot vinaigrette and each lend their own flavor and texture to the bowl. Then, baked tofu, crispy chickpeas, seasoned butter beans, cherry tomatoes and avocados are arranged across the top for a fully satisfying meal.

Make the crispy chickpeas ahead of time so that this salad comes together quickly. Store them in a sealed container and they will last forever.

Crispy Chickpeas

1 tbsp (15 ml) tamari

1 tbsp (15 ml) sunflower oil

1 tbsp (15 ml) freshly squeezed lemon juice

1 tbsp (8 g) nutritional yeast

1½ cups (300 g) cooked or 1 (15-oz [425-g]) can chickpeas, drained, skins removed and dried

Baked Tofu

1 tbsp (15 ml) sunflower oil

1 tbsp (8 g) nutritional yeast

1 tsp tamari

½ tsp turmeric

½ tsp kala namak

7.5 oz (213 g) extra firm tofu, pressed for 10 minutes and cut into small cubes

Seasoned Butter Beans

1½ cups (300 g) cooked or 1 (15-oz [425-g]) can butter beans, drained

1 tbsp (15 ml) good olive oil

Pinch of salt and a dash of pepper

To make the chickpeas, preheat the oven to 350°F (175°C, or gas mark 4). Line a half sheet pan with parchment paper.

Add the tamari, oil, lemon juice and nutritional yeast to a small bowl. Whisk to combine. Pour the marinade over the chickpeas and toss well to coat. Turn out onto the sheet pan and bake for 1 hour, until the chickpeas start to look dry. Turn off the oven and let the chickpeas sit in the oven for at least 2 hours to be sure they are all completely dry and crispy.

To make the tofu, preheat the oven to 350°F (175°C, or gas mark 4). Line a half sheet pan with parchment paper.

Add the oil, nutritional yeast, tamari, turmeric and kala namak to a medium mixing bowl. Whisk together. Add the tofu to the bowl and toss to coat the tofu well. Arrange the tofu in a single layer on the sheet pan and bake for 30 minutes, until brown and crispy.

To make the seasoned butter beans, gently toss them with oil, salt and pepper, coating the beans well.

(Continued)

Cobb Salad (Continued)

Lemon–Shallot Vinaigrette

1 small shallot, diced small

2 tbsp (30 ml) freshly squeezed lemon juice

2 tbsp (30 ml) white balsamic vinegar

¼ cup (60 ml) good olive oil

1 tbsp (15 ml) golden maple syrup

½ tsp salt

Salad

1 head romaine lettuce, chopped into small pieces

2 bunches watercress, stems trimmed and cut into pieces

2 heads of endive, cut into small pieces

12 cherry tomatoes, halved

1 avocado, peeled, pitted and cut into cubes

2 tbsp (6 g) thinly sliced chives

To make the lemon–shallot vinaigrette, add the shallot to a glass jar with a lid or to a dressing bottle. Cover with the lemon juice and vinegar, and let sit for 15 minutes to macerate. Add the oil, maple syrup and salt. Cover the container and shake well to combine. The dressing will separate, so shake well before using.

To assemble the salad, add the romaine, watercress and endive to a big mixing bowl. Toss with about three-quarters of the dressing. Split the dressed greens between two big salad plates. Place the crispy chickpeas on top of the lettuces, making a row across the middle of the plate. Make a row of tomatoes on one side of the chickpeas and a row of avocados on the other. Then add rows of tofu and seasoned beans on the ends. Sprinkle with chives and drizzle with the rest of the dressing.

Cauliflower Po' Boys

with Chipotle Remoulade

Makes 4

Cauliflower is such a versatile vegetable. When seasoned well, it becomes a vehicle for all sorts of vegan twists on old favorites. In this case, it's the Louisiana po' boy, that legendary Southern sandwich, that is so famous there's even an annual festival where chefs compete to win the Best Po' award. This version is so good, I think it would have a shot at winning!

The cauliflower is jazzed up with a mix of spices that scream New Orleans. It's baked, and then it's piled up on a crusty-on-the-outside-soft-on-the-inside French bread roll with spicy chipotle remoulade, shredded lettuce and juicy tomatoes. It is so good, you might find yourself dipping any leftover cauliflower into any extra remoulade even after you finish your meal.

Spiced Cauliflower

1 small head of cauliflower, cut into bite-sized florets
2 tbsp (30 ml) sunflower oil
1 tsp Old Bay seasoning
1 tsp garlic powder
1 tsp onion powder
1 tsp fresh thyme
½ tsp dried oregano
½ tsp chipotle powder
¼ tsp salt
⅛ tsp white pepper

Chipotle Remoulade

½ cup (120 ml) vegan mayo
2 tbsp (30 g) diced pickles
1 tbsp (9 g) capers, drained
1 scallion, thinly sliced
1 tbsp (4 g) chopped fresh parsley
1 tsp mellow white miso
1 tsp minced chipotle in adobo
Pinch of salt

Po' Boys

4 French bread rolls, toasted
Shredded lettuce
4 vine-ripened tomatoes, sliced

To prepare the cauliflower, preheat the oven to 400°F (200°C, or gas mark 6). Line a half sheet pan with parchment paper.

Add the cauliflower to the sheet pan. Drizzle with oil and toss to coat.

In a small bowl, combine the Old Bay, garlic powder, onion powder, thyme, oregano, chipotle powder, salt and pepper. Sprinkle over the cauliflower and toss again to coat. Arrange the cauliflower in a single layer and bake for 30 minutes, until the bottom sides of the florets have caramelized, and they are fork tender.

To make the remoulade, place the mayo, pickles, capers, scallion, parsley, miso and chipotle in a small mixing bowl. Mix well. Season with salt. Use immediately, or store in a sealed container in the refrigerator for up to 1 week.

To assemble the po' boys, spread the chipotle remoulade on the toasted rolls. Layer with lettuce, tomatoes and cauliflower. Cover with the top of the roll and serve.

Roasted Bell Pepper and Ricotta Crostini

Makes 16

You need a good appetizer in your vegan repertoire so look no further than these crostini. Everyone loves a little cheese at a party, right? Serve these little toasts with creamy ricotta, silky roasted peppers and sweet balsamic reduction. They hit on all the flavor and texture notes, plus everyone will be impressed with your kitchen skills.

You probably won't use all of the balsamic reduction for these crostini. Store it in an airtight container, and use it whenever you are looking for a sweet, syrupy addition to a dish. It is especially delicious drizzled over strawberry shortcakes (page 135).

Roasted Bell Peppers
1 small red bell pepper
1 small orange bell pepper
1 small yellow bell pepper

Balsamic Reduction
2 cups (480 ml) balsamic vinegar

Crostini
1 baguette, cut into ¼-inch (6-mm) rounds, about 16 slices
½ cup (114 g) Almond Ricotta (page 169)
2 tsp (10 ml) good olive oil
Pinch of salt
Microgreens

To roast the peppers, place them on a half sheet pan. Bake in a 475°F (240°C, or gas mark 9) oven for 30 to 35 minutes, until the skins of the peppers are charred. Take the peppers out of the oven, place into a heatproof bowl, and cover with plastic wrap. Let stand until they are totally deflated and cool to the touch. Peel the skins, and discard the stems and seeds. Thinly slice the peppers into ribbons. Use right away or store in an airtight container in the refrigerator for up to 1 week.

To make the balsamic reduction, pour the balsamic vinegar into a small saucepan. Simmer over medium-low heat for 25 to 30 minutes, until the vinegar has reduced by half and coats the back of a spoon. Be careful, the vinegar bubbles up as it is cooking.

To make the crostini, preheat the oven to 350°F (175°C, or gas mark 4). Toast the baguette slices on a baking sheet until nice and toasty, about 10 minutes.

To prepare the ricotta, add the ricotta, oil and salt to a mixing bowl. Use a silicone spoonula to fold everything together. Mix until combined. Spread the ricotta on the toasts. Top with microgreens, a pile of pepper ribbons and a drizzle of balsamic reduction.

Deli Chickpea Salad Sandwich

Makes 2

When I was in elementary school, my mother always sent tuna sandwiches for lunch, accompanied by a little note on which she always drew funny people with crazy hair. Sitting at the long tables in the basement cafeteria, I quickly learned that a bunch of potato chips stuffed into the sandwich made for the tastiest bite ever. When I became vegan, I just had to re-create my mom's recipe. It was super easy to do, using chickpeas to sub for tuna and mixing in all of the original flavors, minus the fishiness. Serve with a big pile of potato chips on the side or in the sandwich, whichever you prefer!

Deli Chickpea Salad

1½ cups (300 g) cooked or 1 (15-oz [425-g]) can chickpeas, drained

1 carrot, shredded, about ¼ cup (28 g)

1 stalk of celery, diced, about ¼ cup (25 g)

½ small red onion, finely diced, about 3 tbsp (30 g)

3 tbsp (45 g) diced pickles

¼ cup (60 ml) vegan mayo

1 tbsp (15 ml) ume plum vinegar

1 tsp freshly squeezed lemon juice

1 tsp Grainy Mustard (page 170)

½ tsp coconut sugar

Pinch of salt

Sandwiches

4 slices of your favorite bread, toasted

Lettuce

Potato chips

Add the chickpeas to the food processor and pulse a few times to break them down. A few whole ones are good for texture.

Turn the chickpeas out into a big mixing bowl. Add the carrot, celery, onion, pickles, mayo, vinegar, lemon juice, mustard, coconut sugar and salt. Mix together.

To assemble the sandwiches, pile the chickpea salad on the toast. Layer with lettuce and sneak in some potato chips. Top with a second piece of toast. Slice and serve.

The Tableside Caesar Salad

Serves 4

I couldn't end this chapter without a Caesar salad, one of the most famous dishes in all of food history and one that every vegan needs in their life. Back in my pre-vegan days, I would order it every time I went out to eat. I especially loved the tableside presentation with the big wooden bowl and the freshly made dressing. It was something I could never imagine making at home, because I could not conceive of ever buying anchovies. Just thinking about them creeps me out, but they do make that dressing pretty tasty. After a lot of experimentation, I realized that the pairing of miso and ume plum vinegar are excellent substitutions for the unctuous umami flavor the anchovies impart. And so, I created a dressing that is a wildly delicious vegan version of the original.

Caesar Dressing

½ cup (120 ml) Cashew Cream (page 165)

2 tbsp (30 ml) good olive oil

2 cloves garlic

2 tbsp (18 g) capers, drained

2 tbsp (30 ml) freshly squeezed lemon juice

2 tsp (11 g) mellow white miso

1 tsp ume plum vinegar

1 tsp Grainy Mustard (page 170)

½ tsp coconut sugar

Pinch of salt

Salad

2 heads of romaine lettuce, chopped into bite-sized pieces

1 cup (30 g) croutons

Fresh pepper

1 Macadamia nut, a few scrapes on a microplane

To make the dressing, add the cashew cream, oil, garlic, capers, lemon juice, miso, vinegar, mustard, coconut sugar and salt to a blender. Blend until smooth. Use immediately, or store in a sealed container in the refrigerator for up to 1 week or in the freezer for up to 3 months. If it has thickened up, add a splash of water and mix well.

To assemble the salad, add the romaine and croutons to a salad bowl. Pour about half of the dressing over top and toss to coat well. Add as much dressing as you like (or all of it, like I do!) and continue tossing until everything is combined. Season with pepper and shaved macadamia.

NOTE:

To make croutons, cut your favorite bread into bite-sized cubes. Toast it in the oven on a half sheet pan lined with parchment paper at 325°F (170°C, or gas mark 3) for 20 to 30 minutes, until completely toasted through. Store in a sealed container.

MAIN DISHES

An alternative name for this chapter could be, "anything they can eat we can eat vegan." From lasagna and tacos to meatballs and steak, plant-based ingredients make old dishes new again—and into the stuff of vegan dreams.

Fettucine Alfredo

Serves 4

It is said that Fettucine Alfredo was invented by Alfredo di Lelio at his restaurant in Rome, in an effort to sweet talk his wife into eating after she gave birth to their son. He presented her with a bowl of fettucine tossed with butter and Parmesan. Who wouldn't want to eat that? I know I would, but it is decidedly not vegan—so what is a girl to do? Reinvent it! The Parmesan is replaced by a creamy sauce made from cashews, pine nuts, miso and ume plum vinegar. And it's tossed with vegan butter for a decadent dish that is quite possibly even more delicious than Mr. di Lelio's!

This makes more sauce than you will need for this recipe. Store the rest in the refrigerator for up to three days or in the freezer for up to three months. If it has thickened up, add a splash of water and mix well.

Alfredo Sauce

1 cup (240 ml) Cashew Cream (page 165)

¼ cup (34 g) pine nuts

2 tbsp (16 g) nutritional yeast

2 tbsp (30 ml) melted refined coconut oil

2 tbsp (30 ml) freshly squeeze lemon juice

1 tbsp (17 g) mellow white miso

1 tbsp (15 ml) ume plum vinegar

1 nutmeg, 10 scrapes on a microplane

Dash of white pepper

Pinch of salt

To Serve

½ lb (226 g) uncooked fettucine

2 tbsp (28 g) vegan butter (page 166)

1 Macadamia nut, a few scrapes on a microplane

To make the Alfredo sauce, add the cashew cream, pine nuts, nutritional yeast, oil, lemon juice, miso, vinegar, nutmeg, pepper and salt to a blender. Blend until smooth.

To make the pasta, bring a large pot of salted water to a boil. Cook the pasta according to the package instructions. Drain the pasta, reserving some of the water, and put the pasta back into the same pot. Add the butter and use tongs to coat the noodles.

Pour about half of the sauce over the pasta and use tongs to mix well. Add a little pasta water to make the sauce silky.

Portion the pasta out into individual serving bowls. Top with shaved macadamia.

The Beet Burger

Makes 12

No vegan cookbook would be complete without a veggie burger. This is my winning formula. It's all about texture; veggie burgers should be firm like their meaty counterparts, so they don't sploosh out the sides of the bun after one bite. Served with special sauce, lettuce, pickles and onions, these burgers will turn anyone into a veggie burger lover!

Beet Burgers

1 cup (124 g) grated zucchini, about 1 regular-sized zucchini

1 tsp of salt, plus a pinch

1 cup (110 g) grated carrot, about 2 regular-sized carrots

1 cup (110 g) grated beets, about 2 regular-sized beets

1 cup (about 35 g) packed fresh spinach

1 cup (67 g) packed baby kale

½ cup (25 g) chopped scallions, white and green parts, about 4 regular-sized scallions

1 cup (117 g) walnuts or pecans

1 cup (138 g) pumpkin seeds

1 cup (102 g) quinoa flakes

Special Sauce

½ cup (120 ml) vegan mayo

3 tbsp (45 g) diced pickles

1 tsp Grainy Mustard (page 170)

1 tsp ketchup

1 tsp apple cider vinegar

1 tsp coconut sugar

½ tsp garlic powder

½ tsp onion powder

½ tsp paprika

Buns and Toppings

Burger buns

Red onion

Pickles

Lettuce

To prepare the zucchini, add the zucchini into a fine-mesh strainer over a bowl. Sprinkle with salt and mix around with a fork. Let stand to drain. Use the fork to press the zucchini against the strainer to release as much water as possible. Set aside.

Add the carrots and beets to a bowl. Add the spinach, kale and scallions to the food processor. Process until finely ground. Add the mixture to the grated vegetables. Add the walnuts and pumpkin seeds to the processor and process until finely ground. Add them to the vegetable mixture. Add the zucchini, quinoa flakes and a pinch of salt. Use your hands to mix everything together really well.

Preheat the oven to 350°F (175°C, or gas mark 4). Line a half sheet pan with parchment paper. Using a ¼-cup (60-ml) measure, scoop out the mixture, forming burgers by really packing the mixture together, and pressing it between your palms. If your hands get sticky, rinse them off in between. Place the burgers onto the sheet pan and bake for 30 minutes, flipping them over at the 15-minute mark.

To make the special sauce, add the mayo, pickles, mustard, ketchup, vinegar, coconut sugar, garlic powder, onion powder and paprika to a small bowl. Mix well. Serve immediately, or store in the refrigerator in a sealed jar for up to 1 week.

To assemble the burgers, toast the buns. Spread the special sauce on both sides. Place a burger on the bottom bun. Layer with onion, pickles and lettuce. Top with the other half of the bun.

Crabless Cakes

Makes 12

The first time I had crab cakes was at a restaurant in Maryland. I was at a business lunch and every single person ordered them. The restaurant served an award-winning version and so I jumped right on that bandwagon and it was a pretty tasty situation. What made it so delicious? The combination of soft crab meat, crunchy vegetables, fresh parsley and Old Bay seasoning. To make them vegan, I trade the crab for hearts of palm and shredded zucchini. I am not kidding when I say that I make these little cakes every single time I have a party, and they always disappear. No one ever misses the crab!

Crabless Cakes

¼ cup (31 g) shredded zucchini

⅛ tsp salt, plus more for seasoning

1 stalk celery, cut into big pieces

1 carrot, cut into big pieces

1 scallion, white and green parts, cut into big pieces

½ small red onion, cut into big pieces

½ small red bell pepper, cut into big pieces

1 big handful of fresh parsley

1 (14-oz [397-g]) can hearts of palm, coarsely chopped

2 tsp (5 g) Old Bay seasoning

¼ cup (60 ml) vegan mayo

1 tbsp (15 ml) Grainy Mustard (page 170)

1 cup (102 g) quinoa flakes

Dash of pepper

Sunflower oil, for cooking

To prepare the zucchini, add the zucchini into a fine-mesh strainer over a bowl. Sprinkle with salt and mix around with a fork. Let stand to drain. Use the fork to press the zucchini against the strainer to release as much water as possible before adding to the vegetable mixture.

Add the celery, carrot, scallion, onion, pepper and parsley to the food processor. Pulse a few times until everything is processed but still has some texture.

Run your knife through the hearts of palm to break them down, leaving some bigger, round pieces. Add them to a big mixing bowl.

Add the vegetables to the hearts of palm. Add the drained zucchini, Old Bay, mayo, mustard and quinoa flakes. Mix well, and season with salt and pepper. Refrigerate for at least 30 minutes.

Preheat the oven to 200°F (93°C, or gas mark ½). Line a plate with paper towels and a half sheet pan with parchment paper.

Take the mixture out of the refrigerator. Heat the oil in a cast-iron or nonstick skillet over medium heat. When it is shimmering, it's time to cook the crabless cakes. Scoop up about 2 tablespoons (30 g) of the mixture and drop it gently onto the oil, pressing the top down ever so slightly. You should get 12 crabless cakes. Cook three to four cakes at a time, without crowding the pan, until the bottom side is brown, about 5 minutes. Carefully flip them over, flattening them just a bit with the spatula, and cook until the bottom side is browned.

(Continued)

Crabless Cakes (Continued)

Garlic and Herb Aioli
½ cup (120 ml) vegan mayo
1 clove garlic, pressed
½ small shallot, finely diced
1 tbsp (9 g) capers, drained
1 tbsp (3 g) chopped chives
1 tbsp (4 g) chopped fresh parsley
1 tbsp (6 g) lemon zest
1 tsp Grainy Mustard (page 170)
Pinch of salt

To Serve
Chives
Lemon wedges

Place the cakes onto the paper towels to absorb the excess oil then transfer to the sheet pan in the oven to keep warm. Add more oil to the pan, if necessary, and continue to cook the rest of the cakes.

To make the aioli, place the mayo, garlic, shallot, capers, chives, parsley, lemon zest and mustard in a small mixing bowl. Mix well. Season with salt. Use immediately, or store in a sealed container in the refrigerator for up to 1 week.

Serve the crabless cakes with aioli, chives and lemon wedges.

Portobello Steaks with Creamed Spinach and Herbed Butter

Serves 2

The typical steak house dinner gets a makeover! Juicy portobello mushrooms are roasted in a delicious marinade of white wine, olive oil and white balsamic vinegar, and they star as the steak in this dish. Cashew cream and shallots turn spinach into a decadent side dish while fresh herbs take vegan butter to the next level. After one bite, this plate of food will change anyone's mind about what constitutes a steak dinner.

Marinated Portobellos

2 tbsp (30 ml) vegan white wine

2 tbsp (30 ml) good olive oil, plus more for brushing

2 tbsp (30 ml) white balsamic vinegar

Pinch of salt and a dash of pepper

4 big portobello mushrooms, stems and gills removed

Creamed Spinach

1 tbsp (15 ml) good olive oil

½ small onion, thinly sliced into half-moons

2 shallots, thinly sliced

1 (5-oz [142-g]) box fresh baby spinach

½ cup (120 ml) Cashew Cream (page 165)

½ cup (120 ml) water

1 nutmeg, 10 scrapes on a microplane

Pinch of salt

Dash of white pepper

Preheat the oven to 400°F (200°C, or gas mark 6). Line a half sheet pan with parchment paper.

Whisk together the wine, oil, vinegar, salt and pepper. Lightly brush the caps of the mushrooms with oil. Place them cap side down, inside side up, on the sheet pan. Fill each portobello evenly with marinade.

Bake the mushrooms for 15 minutes, until tender and the juices are flowing. Remove them from the oven and let them rest. Slice the mushrooms into thick pieces, reserving any excess marinade.

In the meantime, to make the spinach, heat the oil in a deep pot over medium-low heat. When the oil is shimmering, add the onion and shallots. Sauté until they are soft and fragrant, about 5 minutes. Add the spinach, cover and cook until the spinach starts to wilt, about 5 minutes. Uncover and use tongs to toss the spinach around until fully wilted. Add the cashew cream, water, nutmeg, salt and pepper. Mix together. Cook for 2 or 3 more minutes to heat the cream all the way through.

(Continued)

Portobello Steaks with Creamed Spinach and Herbed Butter (Continued)

Herbed Butter

1 tsp thinly sliced chives

1 tsp minced fresh dill

1 tsp minced fresh parsley

¼ cup (56 g) vegan butter (page 166), softened

Pinch of salt

To make the herbed butter, mix the chives, dill and parsley into the butter. Season with salt.

To assemble your steak dinner, divide the sliced portobellos and creamed spinach between two plates. Pour any excess marinade over the top. Serve with a small scoop of herbed butter.

NOTE:

Even though wine is made from grapes, it may be processed using animal products. It happens during the fining stage, which is when winemakers clarify and stabilize the wine. Traditionally, this is done using things such as casein (milk protein), albumin (egg whites), chitin (crustacean shells), gelatin (boiled animal parts) and isinglass (fish bladders). Vegan or not, that all sounds kind of gross. Luckily, there are a lot of winemakers using fining agents that are vegan friendly; things such as bentonite clay, activated charcoal and limestone. Ask the people at the liquor store or check out Barnivore.com to find a good bottle.

Heirloom Tomato, Caramelized Onion and Ricotta Galette

Makes 8 slices

Galettes are rustic tarts and really easy to make. If you haven't guessed by now, that's kind of a theme in my kitchen! Galettes can be filled with almost anything—sweet or savory. This one is a re-creation of one of my all-time faves, a galette I used to order at a restaurant out on the east end of Long Island. What made it special was the fresh creamy ricotta and buttery caramelized onions combined with tangy heirloom tomatoes. With the simple swap of ricotta, I can have this any time I want! I particularly love colorful heirlooms; if you can't find them, use the prettiest tomatoes you can find, such as vine-ripened ones or even a bunch of cute little cherry tomatoes. Honestly, any tomato works and the result will be both delicious and beautiful.

Caramelized Onions

1 tsp good olive oil

1 big sweet white onion, thinly sliced into half-moons

1 clove garlic

Pinch of salt

Galette Dough

1 recipe The Little Pie Crust (page 181)

Filling

¼ cup (57 g) Almond Ricotta (page 169)

1 tsp good olive oil, plus more for drizzling

1 tsp fresh thyme

Pinch of salt

2 or 3 colorful heirloom tomatoes, sliced

Heat a heavy bottomed pan with sides over medium-low heat. Add the oil. When it is shimmering, add the onion. Use tongs to mix the onion around and coat it with the oil. Cover the pan and sweat the onion, until it becomes translucent and starts to soften, about 8 minutes.

Uncover and add the garlic and salt. Stir around. Continue to cook, uncovered, over medium-low heat, stirring every so often, until the onion is golden and buttery, 20 to 25 minutes. If the onion starts to stick to the pan, add a little bit of water. Take it off the heat and set aside.

Preheat the oven to 400°F (200°C, or gas mark 6). Line a half sheet pan with parchment paper.

Roll out the dough to about 12 inches (30 cm) around and ⅛-inch (3-mm) thick. Lift it up and flip it over onto the sheet pan.

To prepare the filling, add the ricotta, oil, thyme and salt to a small mixing bowl. Use a silicone spoonula to fold everything together. Mix until combined.

(Continued)

Heirloom Tomato, Caramelized Onion and Ricotta Galette (Continued)

Glaze

1 tbsp (20 g) thick apricot preserves

2 tbsp (30 ml) water

Spread the ricotta into a thin layer on the dough, leaving a 1½-inch (3.5-cm) border of dough. Arrange the caramelized onion on top of the ricotta. Arrange the tomatoes on top of the onion in a pleasing way, and top with a generous drizzle of oil.

Fold the edges of the dough over the filling, pleating it as you go around. If it tears, just pinch it back together.

To make the glaze, whisk the apricot preserves with the water. Brush the glaze over the edges and top the folded dough.

Bake for 40 to 45 minutes, until the crust is golden brown, and the tomatoes look soft and wilted. Let stand for 10 minutes before cutting into it. Serve warm or at room temperature.

Four Alarm Three Bean Chili

Serves 4

Chili is a fantastic, easy-to-make, one-pot meal that can be served myriad ways—over rice, French fries, baked potatoes or on a big pile of tortilla chips for souped-up nachos. And there is absolutely no need for any meat! This vegan chili is just as filling as anything you have ever eaten, with three kinds of beans seasoned with eight different spices including Mexican oregano, smoky chipotle powder, cocoa powder and cinnamon. It's a deeply flavorful pot of goodness that tastes even better the next day. Make it ahead of time and have a hearty, spicy, protein-packed meal at the ready.

Chili

1 tbsp (15 ml) sunflower oil

1 small onion, diced

1 clove garlic, pressed

1 jalapeño, seeds and ribs removed, diced

¼ tsp crushed red pepper flakes

A few big pinches of salt

2 carrots, sliced into thin rounds

½ red bell pepper, diced

½ orange bell pepper, diced

½ yellow bell pepper, diced

2 tbsp (16 g) nutritional yeast

1 tsp chili powder

1 tsp coriander

1 tsp Mexican oregano

1 tsp cumin

½ tsp chipotle powder

½ tsp cocoa powder

¼ tsp cinnamon

2 tbsp (32 g) tomato paste

(Continued)

To make the chili, heat a big pot over medium-low heat and add the oil. When it is shimmering, add the onion. Cook until the onion is translucent, 3 or 4 minutes. Add the garlic, jalapeño, red pepper flakes and salt. Cook until the garlic is fragrant, about 1 minute.

Add the carrots and bell peppers, and sauté for 5 minutes, until the vegetables start to soften. Add the nutritional yeast, chili powder, coriander, Mexican oregano, cumin, chipotle powder, cocoa powder and cinnamon. Stir around to coat the vegetables. Add the tomato paste and use a wooden spoon to mix it around, cooking it for 3 to 4 minutes.

(Continued)

Four Alarm Three Bean Chili (Continued)

1 cup (194 g) black beans
1 cup (184 g) kidney beans
1 cup (194 g) pinto beans
1 cup (136 g) frozen or canned corn
1 (14-oz [397-g]) can tomato sauce
1 cup (240 ml) water
1 tbsp (15 ml) freshly squeezed lime juice

Avocado Mash

1 avocado
1 scallion, thinly sliced
2 tbsp (30 ml) freshly squeezed lime juice
Pinch of salt

Sour Cream

¼ cup (60 ml) Cashew Cream (page 165)
1 tbsp (15 ml) freshly squeezed lime juice
Pinch of salt

Toppings

Toasted pumpkin seeds
Lime wedges

Add the beans, corn and tomato sauce to the pot. Add the water to the can and swirl it around so that you get the rest of whatever is left and stir it into the vegetables.

Bring to a high simmer, cover, and cook for 25 to 30 minutes until everything is seasoned and heated through. When the chili is done cooking, add the lime juice.

To make the avocado mash, add the flesh of the avocado to a small mixing bowl. Add the scallion, lime juice and salt. Mash the avocado with the back of a fork pressing against the side of the bowl. Mix everything together.

To make the sour cream, mix together the cashew cream, lime juice and salt.

To toast the pumpkin seeds, preheat the oven to 350°F (175°C, or gas mark 4). Line a quarter sheet pan with parchment paper. Arrange the pumpkin seeds in a single layer and bake for 10 to 15 minutes, until the seeds start to brown.

Serve the chili with avocado mash, sour cream, toasted pumpkin seeds and lime wedges.

NOTE:

A can of beans yields about 1½ cups (about 300 g) which is more than this recipe calls for. But don't waste them; freeze them for up to 3 months.

Lentil Bolognese

Makes about 2½ cups (about 560 g)

Traditional Bolognese sauce can take up three hours, but this version cooks up in about a third of the time and the result is just as delicious as anything you have ever tasted. This protein-packed sauce is made with brown and red lentils. Brown lentils are earthy and hearty and add big texture, while red lentils add a hint of sweetness as they disappear into the sauce and thicken it up. Seasoned with traditional Italian flavors, some crushed red pepper flakes and white wine, this sauce is perfect for a family-style pasta dinner. Serve tossed with big, fat noodles such as pappardelle or rigatoni.

2 tbsp (30 ml) good olive oil

1 small onion, finely diced

1 big carrot, finely diced

2 stalks celery, finely diced

2 cloves garlic, pressed

1 tsp Italian seasoning

¼ tsp crushed red pepper flakes

Pinch of salt

½ cup (120 ml) vegan white wine

¾ cup (144 g) brown lentils

¼ cup (48 g) red lentils

3 cups (720 ml) water

1 cup (240 ml) All-Purpose Red Sauce (page 173)

½ cup (120 ml) cashew milk (page 174)

1 tsp sherry vinegar

Heat the oil in a big sauté pan over medium-low heat. Add the onion, carrot, celery, garlic, Italian seasoning, red pepper flakes and salt. Cook, stirring occasionally, until the vegetables are tender, about 15 minutes.

Add the wine. Bring to a high simmer and cook until the wine has almost evaporated, about 5 minutes.

Add the brown lentils, red lentils, water and sauce. Bring to a boil, reduce to a simmer and cook for 50 minutes to 1 hour until the sauce has thickened and the lentils are completely tender.

Stir in the milk and cook for 5 more minutes. Take the pan off the heat, stir in the sherry vinegar and let stand for 30 minutes to allow the flavors to meld. If not using right away, store in the refrigerator for up to 3 days or in the freezer for up to 3 months.

Shiitake Asada Tacos
with Corn Salsa

Makes 6

I am a true believer in Taco Tuesday. Literally, I make tacos every Tuesday for dinner. A perfect taco consists of a marinated centerpiece, topped with a flavorful salsa, topped with some crunchy, raw vegetables, all tucked into warm corn tortillas. In this variation, shiitakes are marinated in citrus, garlic, chili pepper and spices cooked right on the stovetop. Make your salsa and heat your tortillas while the shiitakes are marinating, because they take almost no time to cook. Dinner will be on the table faster than you can say "Taco Tuesday!"

Shiitake Asada

¼ cup (60 ml) freshly squeezed lime juice

2 tbsp (30 ml) freshly squeezed orange juice

1 clove garlic, pressed

½ small serrano, ribs and seeds removed, diced

1 tsp chili powder

1 tsp coriander

1 tsp cumin

4 cups (198 g) shiitake mushrooms, stems removed and thinly sliced

2 tbsp (30 ml) sunflower oil

Pinch of salt

Corn Salsa

1 cup (154 g) fresh or canned corn

2 tbsp (20 g) finely diced red onion

½ small serrano, ribs and seeds removed, diced

1 tbsp (15 ml) freshly squeezed lime juice

2 tsp (scant 1 g) chopped fresh cilantro

2 tsp (4 g) chopped fresh mint

Pinch of salt

To Serve

12 corn tortillas

1 avocado, peeled, pitted and mashed

Lime wedges

To prepare the mushrooms, whisk together the lime juice, orange juice, garlic, serrano, chili powder, coriander, cumin and salt in a medium mixing bowl. Add the mushrooms, mix around to coat and marinate for 30 minutes.

To make the corn salsa, add the corn, onion, serrano, lime juice, cilantro, mint and salt to a small mixing bowl. Mix together. Set aside.

To prepare the tortillas, char them one at a time on an open flame or heat them on a dry cast-iron skillet.

Heat a cast-iron or nonstick skillet over medium heat. Add the oil. When it is shimmering, add the mushrooms and marinade. Cook until the liquid is absorbed, about 5 minutes.

To assemble the tacos, double up the tortillas. Layer with mushrooms, avocado and corn salsa. Serve with lime wedges.

NOTE:

Personally, I think cilantro tastes like soap, so I add mint to any recipe that calls for it. The fresh, sweet and cooling flavor of mint amps up the citrus flavor in the cilantro making it much more pleasant to eat.

Chickpea Scampi

Serves 4

The night before I became a full-fledged vegan, I made myself a big bowl of shrimp scampi. I ate the whole thing myself and said goodbye to animal products forever. It didn't take long to figure out how to veganize scampi; all I had to do was follow my original recipe and make two substitutions. The sauce was easy—thank goodness for vegan butter—but I had to find something to stand in for the shrimp. Enter chickpeas, an absolutely delicious proxy. When coated in the sauce, there is no missing the shrimp.

This is a quick and easy meal that comes together in the time it takes to boil the pasta. Serve with a glass of wine, a salad and crusty bread, and call it a night!

½ lb (226 g) uncooked orecchiette

¼ cup (60 ml) good olive oil

¼ cup (56 g) vegan butter (page 166)

3 cloves garlic, pressed

1 cup (240 ml) vegan white wine

Pinch of salt and a dash of pepper

1½ cups (300 g) cooked or 1 (15-oz [425-g]) can chickpeas, drained

2 tbsp (30 ml) freshly squeezed lemon juice

Handful of chopped fresh parsley

To prepare the pasta, bring a large pot of salted water to a boil. Cook the pasta according to the package instructions. Drain the pasta, reserving some of the water, and put the pasta back into the same pot.

To make the sauce, heat a big pan with sides over medium-low heat. Add the oil and butter, and melt them together. Turn the heat to low and add the garlic. Sauté until fragrant, about 2 minutes. Add the wine, salt and pepper, and bring up to a simmer. Cook until the wine reduces by half and the sauce starts to thicken, about 5 minutes.

Add the chickpeas to the pan and toss them around to coat with the sauce. Cook for 5 minutes to heat them through. Add the orecchiette to the pan, and use a spoon to toss the pasta around and coat with the sauce. Add a little pasta water to make the sauce silky. Squeeze lemon juice over the top and toss one more time.

Portion out into individual serving bowls and top with parsley.

Lobster Mushroom Mac 'n' Cheese

Serves 4 to 6

Mac 'n' cheese is like the Holy Grail of vegan cooking, a must-have on every vegan restaurant's menu and in every vegan home because we all need a little pasta and cheese in our lives. But this is no ordinary mac 'n' cheese. It's a classy, sophisticated version that is elevated with the addition of lobster mushrooms, probably the most fun plant-based proxy in this book! They are orangish-reddish in color, kind of look like cooked lobster meat and have a faint seafood-esque flavor. Mixed with an extra-decadent cheese sauce made with roasted garlic, this basic casserole is not so basic. Make it on date night and serve it with a glass of champagne!

Lobster Mushrooms

1 oz (28 g) dried lobster mushrooms, soaked overnight

Cheese Sauce

1 cup (240 ml) Cashew Cream (page 165)

2 tbsp (30 ml) melted refined coconut oil

2 tbsp (30 ml) ume plum vinegar

2 tbsp (16 g) nutritional yeast

1 tbsp (15 g) mashed roasted garlic, (see note on page 42)

1 tbsp (15 ml) freshly squeezed lemon juice

1 tbsp (17 g) mellow white miso

Pinch of salt

To prepare the mushrooms, lift them out of the soaking liquid, squeezing them as you go, and add them to a strainer. Rinse the mushrooms to remove any grit. Chop into bite-sized pieces and set aside.

Strain the soaking liquid through a paper towel and set aside.

To prepare the pasta, bring a large pot of salted water to a boil. Cook the pasta according to the package instructions. Drain the pasta, reserving some of the water, and put the pasta back into the same pot.

To make the cheese sauce, add cashew cream, oil, vinegar, nutritional yeast, roasted garlic, lemon juice, miso and salt to a blender. Blend until smooth. The cheese sauce can be made ahead of time and stored in the refrigerator for up to 3 days or in the freezer for up to 3 months. If it has thickened up, add a splash of water and mix well.

Preheat the oven to 350°F (175°C, or gas mark 4). Place a 1¾-quart (1.6-L) baking dish on top of a half sheet pan.

(Continued)

Lobster Mushroom Mac 'n' Cheese (Continued)

Mac 'n' Cheese

½ lb (226 g) uncooked cavatappi

1½ tbsp (8 ml) good olive oil, divided

3 shallots, thinly sliced

¼ cup (60 ml) mushroom soaking liquid, strained well

¾ cup (180 ml) water

2 tbsp (16 g) Seasoned Breadcrumbs (page 178)

Heat a cast-iron or nonstick skillet over medium-low heat. Add 1 tablespoon oil. When it starts shimmering, add the shallots and salt, and cook until translucent, about 5 minutes.

Add the chopped mushrooms to the shallots and stir around. Add the mushroom soaking liquid and water and bring to a high simmer. Cook low, slow and uncovered, stirring occasionally, until the liquid has almost evaporated and the mushrooms are soft, about 30 minutes.

Pour the mushroom-shallot mixture and cheese sauce over the pasta. Use tongs to gently mix everything together. Add a little pasta water to make the sauce silky.

Pour the entire mixture into the baking dish.

In a small mixing bowl, combine the breadcrumbs and ½ tablespoon oil, working it all together until the oil is completely incorporated into the breadcrumbs. Sprinkle on top of the mac 'n' cheese.

Bake for 30 minutes, until the top looks crispy and the sauce is bubbling. Let stand for at least 10 minutes to cool slightly.

NOTE:

Dried mushrooms can be found in the market or ordered online. They are easy to reconstitute, but there is some difference of opinion on whether or not to use the soaking liquid for cooking. On the pro side, the liquid is full of flavor. On the con side, there may be some grit left over. Not one to waste a thing in the kitchen, I recommend straining the liquid through a paper towel and using it in the sauce. If you are concerned, strain it twice—or leave it out and substitute water or vegetable stock.

Baked Spicy BBQ Tempeh
and Creamy Slaw

Serves 4

When it comes to barbecue, there is nothing more important than the sauce. Does it matter what it is slathered all over? I don't think so! There are all different styles, but this one is like a cross between a Kansas City sauce and a St. Louis sauce. It's thick, sticky, tangy, sweet and spicy all at the same time. You don't need an actual barbecue to make this dish; just brush it over some tempeh and bake it. Serve it with this colorful, cooling slaw and some rolls on the side for a barbecue any time of the year!

BBQ Tempeh

1 (8-oz [226-g]) package soy tempeh, thinly sliced the short way, about 24 pieces
2 tbsp (30 ml) water
2 tbsp (30 ml) tamari
2 tbsp (30 ml) apple cider vinegar
2 tbsp (30 ml) sunflower oil
2 tbsp (32 g) tomato paste
2 tbsp (18 g) coconut sugar
1 tsp garlic powder
1 tsp onion powder
1 tsp mustard powder
1 tsp paprika
½ tsp cayenne pepper

To make the tempeh, place the tempeh in a pot and cover with water. Bring to a boil. Reduce the heat and simmer and cook, uncovered, for 10 minutes.

Preheat the oven to 350°F (175°C, or gas mark 4). Line a half sheet pan with parchment paper.

In a small mixing bowl, whisk together the water, tamari, vinegar, oil, tomato paste, coconut sugar, garlic powder, onion powder, mustard powder, paprika and cayenne pepper.

When the tempeh has finished simmering, lift it out of the water with tongs, and gently dip it into the sauce, flipping it over to coat both sides. Place the tempeh on the sheet pan, reserving the remaining sauce. Bake for 25 to 30 minutes, until the tempeh starts to brown and the sauce starts to look dry.

Add the reserved sauce to a small saucepan and heat on low. When the tempeh is done, remove it from the oven and brush the warm sauce over the top of the tempeh.

(Continued)

Creamy Slaw

2 cups (140 g) shredded purple cabbage

1 cup (110 g) shredded carrot

4 scallions, white and green parts, thinly sliced

1 cup (154 g) fresh, defrosted frozen, or canned corn

2 tbsp (8 g) chopped fresh parsley

½ cup (120 ml) vegan mayo

1 tsp lime zest

2 tbsp (30 ml) freshly squeezed lime juice

1 tbsp (9 g) coconut sugar

Big pinch of salt

Sides

Soft rolls

In the meantime, make the slaw by combining the cabbage, carrot, scallions, corn and parsley in a big mixing bowl. Add the mayo, lime zest, lime juice and coconut sugar. Mix well, coating the vegetables. Season with salt. Let stand while the tempeh is baking, to let the cabbage soften and the flavors meld.

Serve the tempeh with the slaw and soft rolls.

Better-Than-Takeout Pad Thai

Serves 2

Pad Thai was my favorite dish to order in on nights I got home too late to cook. When I really got into vegan cooking, it became one of my biggest challenges to re-create. The main ingredient is fish sauce, a fermented, salty, condiment used in Thai cuisine, that is famous for its ability to impart umami, that unique savory flavor that makes food taste really, really good. Just like in The Tableside Caesar Salad (page 67), the pairing of miso and ume plum vinegar do the trick. When combined with the rest of the ingredients, this meal is a way better option than takeout any day of the week. Not only that, but it comes together in less time than it takes to get delivery.

Pad Thai

4 oz (113 g) uncooked Pad Thai noodles

2 tbsp (30 ml) tamari

2 tbsp (34 g) mellow white miso

2 tbsp (30 ml) ume plum vinegar

1 tbsp (15 ml) dark maple syrup

1 tbsp (15 ml) sunflower oil

½ small onion, thinly sliced into half-moons

1 cup (70 g) sliced shiitake mushrooms

1 clove garlic, pressed

½ tsp crushed red pepper flakes

1 big carrot, shredded

2 baby bok choy, chopped

¼–½ cup (60–120 ml) water

Toppings

Handful of bean sprouts

2 scallions, green and white parts, thinly sliced

2 tbsp (18 g) ground peanuts

2 wedges of lime

To prepare the noodles, bring a large pot of water to a boil. Cook the noodles according to the package instructions. Drain the noodles, run them under cold water and set aside.

To make the sauce, whisk together the tamari, miso, vinegar and maple syrup. Set aside.

To prepare the vegetables, heat a cast-iron or nonstick skillet over medium heat. Add the oil. When it is shimmering, add the onion and mushrooms. Cook until the onion is just translucent and the mushrooms are starting to soften, about 8 minutes. Add the garlic and red pepper flakes. Cook for 1 to 2 minutes, until fragrant.

Add the carrot and bok choy. Cook until the bok choy is starting to wilt. Add the sauce and ¼ cup (60 ml) of water, and toss with the vegetables. Cook until the bok choy is fully wilted and bright green and the sauce is bubbling, about 5 minutes.

Add the noodles to the vegetables and sauce. Add another ¼ cup (60 ml) of water if the sauce is too thick. Use tongs to toss until everything is mixed together.

Portion out into individual serving bowls and top with bean sprouts, scallions, peanuts and lime wedges.

Savory Roasted Asparagus-Filled Crepes

with Dilly Cream

Makes 6

Savory crepes are often filled with various meats, but there is absolutely no reason for that. At all. Remember the sweet crepes in the breakfast chapter? With the addition of fresh herbs and lemon zest, they are turned into a savory version of themselves. They can be filled with almost anything, but here roasted asparagus are the vegetable star of the show. Topped with a drizzle of cream seasoned with fresh dill, they are a pretty addition to any spring holiday table!

Roasted Asparagus
1 lb (454 g) asparagus spears
1 tbsp (15 ml) good olive oil
¼ tsp salt

Crepes
½ cup (46 g) chickpea flour
2 tbsp (16 g) arrowroot starch/flour
1 cup (240 ml) unsweetened soy milk
1 tsp fresh lemon zest
1 tsp minced parsley
1 tsp minced chives
Pinch of salt
Vegan butter (page 166)

Preheat the oven to 400°F (200°C, or gas mark 6). Line a half sheet pan with parchment paper.

To prepare the asparagus, hold the end of each spear and bend it. It will snap off at the natural point between edible and woody. If the asparagus are very thick, use a vegetable peeler to peel the bottom third of the spear so a little of the white flesh is exposed, for extra tenderness.

Spread the asparagus out on the sheet pan in a single layer. Drizzle with oil. Toss them around to coat the spears and sprinkle with salt. Roast for 15 to 20 minutes, until the asparagus are tender and the tips start to look charred.

To make the crepes, add the chickpea flour and arrowroot to a medium mixing bowl. Whisk to combine. Add the milk, lemon zest, parsley, chives and salt. Whisk together until completely smooth.

Heat a cast-iron griddle or nonstick pan over medium heat, and add a dollop of butter. As it sizzles, use a spatula to coat the entire pan.

(Continued)

Savory Roasted Asparagus–Filled Crepes with Dilly Cream (Continued)

Dilly Cream

¼ cup (60 ml) Cashew Cream (page 165)

1 tbsp (4 g) chopped fresh dill

1 tbsp (15 ml) freshly squeezed lemon juice

Pinch of salt

Scoop up a scant ¼-cup (60-ml) measure of batter and pour it onto the pan. Quickly pick the pan up, tip it gently and rotate it around to distribute the crepe batter into a thin circle. Return to the heat and cook until the edges start to brown, and the top looks dry. Carefully flip the crepe over and cook the other side for another minute. When the first crepe is done, gently place it on a big plate. Cook the remaining crepes and pile them on the plate, covering them with a towel, until all the batter is gone.

To make the dilly cream, mix the cashew cream, dill, lemon juice and salt together.

To assemble the crepes, layer each crepe with asparagus on the side closest to you. Roll it over itself and place it seam side down on the plate. Continue until all of the crepes are filled. Top with a drizzle of dilly cream.

Baja Tacos
with Salsa Fresca and Chipotle Cream

Makes 6

Baja-style fish tacos originated in Baja California, Mexico. All along the coastline of the peninsula, there are taco stands that offer up different variations, depending on the catch of the day. But you don't have to go fishing, you just have to open a package of tofu and season it up with Old Bay, that famous spice combo of celery salt, red pepper, black pepper and paprika that is traditionally used on seafood.

To round it out, these tacos are topped with salsa fresca and chipotle cream and served with wedges of lime. Because no matter what's in a Baja taco, it's mandatory to spritz fresh lime juice over the top right before eating.

Baja Tofu

1 tbsp (15 ml) sunflower oil

1 tbsp (15 ml) tamari

2 tsp (5 g) Old Bay seasoning

½ tsp Mexican oregano

Pinch of salt and a dash of pepper

7.5 oz (213 g) extra firm tofu, pressed for 10 minutes and cut into strips

Salsa Fresca

1 big vine-ripened tomato, seeded and chopped

2 tbsp (20 g) finely diced red onion

½ small serrano, ribs and seeds removed, diced

1 tbsp (15 ml) freshly squeezed lime juice

2 tsp (scant 1 g) chopped fresh cilantro

2 tsp (4 g) chopped fresh mint

Pinch of salt

To make the tofu, preheat the oven to 350°F (175°C, or gas mark 4). Line a half sheet pan with parchment paper.

Add the oil, tamari, Old Bay and Mexican oregano to a medium mixing bowl. Whisk together, and season with salt and pepper. Add the tofu to the bowl and toss to coat the tofu well. Arrange the tofu in a single layer on the sheet pan and bake for 30 minutes.

To make the salsa fresca, add the tomatoes, onion, serrano, lime juice, cilantro, mint and salt to a small mixing bowl. Mix together. Set aside.

(Continued)

Baja Tacos with Salsa Fresca and Chipotle Cream (Continued)

Chipotle Cream

¼ cup (60 ml) Cashew Cream (page 165)

1 tsp chipotle in adobo, minced

1 tbsp (15 ml) freshly squeezed lime juice

Pinch of salt

To Serve

12 corn tortillas

Handful of shredded purple or green cabbage

1 radish, thinly sliced on a mandoline

1 avocado, peeled, pitted and diced

Lime wedges

To make the chipotle cream, mix the cashew cream, chipotle in adobo, lime juice and salt together.

To prepare the tortillas, char them one at a time on an open flame or heat them on a dry cast-iron skillet.

To assemble the tacos, double up the tortillas. Layer with cabbage, tofu, salsa fresca, chipotle cream, radishes and avocado. Serve with lime wedges.

Spicy Pasta Bake

Serves 4 to 6

When I first became vegan, I hated kale. But, since kale is probably the healthiest, most nutrient-dense, leafy green vegetable on the planet, I had to figure out a way to make it taste good. Cue this spicy pasta bake. All of the other flavors take over, so the kale is just there for decoration and nutritional value. This dish will turn any kale hater into a kale lover, promise!

½ lb (226 g) uncooked ziti rigati or rigatoni

2½ tbsp (38 ml) good olive oil, divided

½ small white onion, thinly sliced into half-moons

1 clove garlic, pressed

¼ tsp crushed red pepper flakes

A few pinches of salt

1 (5-oz [142-g]) box baby kale

1 cup (136 g) frozen corn

1 cup (228 g) Almond Ricotta (page 169)

1½ cups (360 ml) All-Purpose Red Sauce (page 173)

1 tbsp (8 g) Seasoned Breadcrumbs (page 178)

1 tbsp (7 g) Almond Parmesan (page 177)

To prepare the pasta, bring a large pot of salted water to a boil. Cook the pasta about 3 minutes less than the package says. Drain the pasta, reserving some of the water, and put the pasta back into the same pot.

To prepare the kale and corn, heat 1 tablespoon (15 ml) of oil in a cast-iron or nonstick pan over medium heat. When the oil is shimmering, add the onion. When it starts to become fragrant and translucent, add the garlic, red pepper flakes and a pinch of salt. Mix around and cook for a minute, until the garlic is fragrant. Add the baby kale and corn. Cook for another minute, until the kale is bright green.

To prepare the ricotta, add the ricotta, 1 tablespoon (15 ml) of oil and a pinch of salt to a small mixing bowl. Use a silicone spoonula to fold everything together. Mix until combined.

Preheat the oven to 350°F (175°C, or gas mark 4). Place a 1¾-quart (1.6-L) baking dish on the top of a half sheet pan. Pour the red sauce over the pasta, mixing gently and allowing the sauce to fill some of the tubes. Fold in about half the ricotta. Add the kale and corn, and mix to distribute everything well. Pour half of the pasta mixture into the baking dish. Use an ice cream scooper or big spoon to dollop almost all of the rest of the ricotta throughout the mixture, saving some for the top. Pour over the rest of the pasta mixture and dollop the last of the ricotta.

In a small mixing bowl, combine the breadcrumbs, Parmesan and ½ tablespoon (8 ml) of oil, working it all together until the oil is completely incorporated into the breadcrumbs and Parmesan. Sprinkle on top of the pasta bake. Cover with foil and bake for 45 minutes. Uncover and cook for another 15 minutes, until the top looks crispy and the sauce is bubbling. Let stand for at least 10 minutes to cool slightly before serving.

Cauliflower Steaks

with Pistachio and Caper Relish

Serves 2

Often, the star of a plate is the sauce or topping, and it is usually smothering steak or chicken. Let's face it, that protein is really just a vehicle for a great sauce. So, one technique I use is to find the right proxy for the meat for my favorite sauce to go on top of.

Well, the vegan world has its own steak—in the form of cauliflower. Whoever came up with that idea is a culinary genius. After the cauliflower is sliced into steaks, it is pan-seared with Aleppo pepper, for a fruity, earthy and mildly spicy flavor, and then finished off in the oven. Then it's time for the topping. Made with white wine, pistachios and capers, it's a nutty mixture that is at once sweet, spicy, salty and delicious.

Cauliflower Steaks

1 big head of cauliflower

1 tbsp (15 ml) good olive oil

1 tsp Aleppo pepper

1 tbsp (15 ml) freshly squeezed lemon juice

Pistachio and Caper Relish

1 tbsp (15 ml) good olive oil

6 scallions, white and green parts, thinly sliced

½ cup (120 ml) white wine

½ cup (62 g) coarsely chopped pistachios

1 tbsp (9 g) capers, drained

1 tbsp (15 ml) sherry vinegar

1 tbsp (15 ml) Grainy Mustard (page 170)

1 tsp fresh thyme

1 tsp coconut sugar

Pinch of salt

Preheat the oven to 400°F (200°C, or gas mark 6). Line a half sheet pan with parchment paper.

To prepare the cauliflower, cut the head in half and then turn the halves cut side down on the cutting board. Next, cut the cauliflower into steaks the short way, resulting in six to eight little steaks.

Heat a cast-iron pan or nonstick pan over medium heat. Add the oil. When it is shimmering, add the cauliflower steaks. Sprinkle the tops with the Aleppo pepper. Cook until the cauliflower starts to look translucent in some areas, about 5 minutes. Use tongs to gently flip the steaks over. Pour the lemon juice over the top of the steaks. Cook the second side for another 5 minutes. Transfer the cauliflower steaks to the sheet pan, leaving the cast-iron pan over the heat. Bake until the steaks start to look charred, about 20 minutes.

To make the relish, carefully add the oil and scallions to the hot pan. Use a wooden spoon to mix them around to coat them with all the pan drippings from the cauliflower, sautéing until they start to become translucent and bright green, about 3 minutes. Deglaze the pan with the wine. Bring it to a boil and reduce to a simmer, until the wine has reduced and thickened up, about 5 minutes. Add the pistachios and capers, and toss to coat with the wine sauce.

In a separate small mixing bowl, whisk together the vinegar, mustard, thyme, coconut sugar and salt. Add the mixture to the pan, mix to incorporate and heat through, about 1 minute.

To assemble, generously top the cauliflower steaks with the relish.

Meatless Meatballs

Makes 15

Meatballs and spaghetti are serious comfort food for me. It was always a good night when my mom called us down to dinner and served up a big pile of pasta and sauce topped with her homemade meatballs. The best part was the char she always managed to achieve on one side of every meatball. In this recipe, the meat is out, and tempeh is in. It's flavored up with Italian seasonings, plus a little miso, nutritional yeast and fresh parsley, for a modern version that is still total comfort food.

1 (8-oz [226-g]) package soy tempeh

1 tbsp (15 ml) tamari

½ cup (120 ml) water

½ tbsp (9 g) mellow white miso

½ tbsp (8 g) tomato paste

1 tsp Italian seasoning

½ tsp onion powder

½ tsp garlic powder

¼ tsp salt

½ cup (64 g) Seasoned Breadcrumbs (page 178)

2 tbsp (16 g) nutritional yeast

1 small handful of chopped fresh parsley

Olive oil, for cooking

Break up the tempeh into big crumbles. Add the tempeh to a pot along with the tamari and water. Bring to a simmer. Every few minutes go in with a wooden spoon in order to break up the tempeh completely. Cook until the liquid is absorbed, about 10 minutes. Let the tempeh cool.

In a small mixing bowl, use a fork to mix the miso and tomato paste together. Add it to the tempeh along with the Italian seasoning, onion powder, garlic powder, salt, breadcrumbs, nutritional yeast and parsley. Use your hands to mix everything together really well.

Preheat the oven to 350°F (175°C, or gas mark 4). Line a quarter sheet pan with parchment paper.

Scoop out about 1 tablespoon (15 ml) of the mixture, forming balls by really packing the mixture together, and rolling it between your palms. If your hands get sticky, rinse them off in between. You should get 15 balls total.

Place the meatballs on the sheet pan and bake for 30 minutes. Cool completely.

At this point, you can store the meatballs in a sealed container in the refrigerator for up to 1 week or in the freezer for up to 3 months. If frozen, defrost when ready to serve.

Heat a small amount of oil in a cast-iron or nonstick skillet over medium heat. When the oil is shimmering, add the meatballs and roll them around to coat with the oil. Cook for a few minutes, allowing one side to get really well done, that famous char, until heated through, about 8 minutes.

Stuffed Shells

with Herbed Ricotta

Makes 15

As you can probably tell by now, I have a lot of food nostalgia, and stuffed shells are an all-time favorite. They always remind me of dinners my family and I used to eat at a restaurant in Little Italy called Grotta Azzurra. We always ended up there after a long day at a museum or some other sight-seeing adventure. Their stuffed shells were epic—jumbo pastas stuffed with creamy ricotta cheese and smothered in red sauce.

The big swap? Vegan ricotta. It doesn't get any easier than this in the kitchen. Plus, these are a real crowd pleaser, so make them for your next party or bring them to your next potluck. I know they will disappear quickly!

15 jumbo shells

1 cup (228 g) Almond Ricotta (page 169)

¼ cup (60 ml) cashew milk (page 174)

2 tbsp (16 g) nutritional yeast

1½ tbsp (23 ml) good olive oil, divided

1 heaping tbsp (4 g) chopped fresh basil

1 heaping tbsp (5 g) chopped fresh parsley

1 heaping tbsp (4 g) chopped fresh chives

1 tsp dried oregano

Pinch of salt

1 cup (240 ml) All-Purpose Red Sauce (page 173)

1 tbsp (8 g) Seasoned Breadcrumbs (page 178)

1 tbsp (7 g) Almond Parmesan (page 177)

To make the shells, bring a large pot of salted water to a boil. Have a quarter sheet pan at the ready. Cook the shells for 10 minutes. Drain them into a colander and run them under cold water, swooshing them around so they don't stick to each other. Quickly lift them out and place them onto the sheet pan.

While the shells are cooking, prepare the filling. In a big mixing bowl, add the ricotta, cashew milk, nutritional yeast, 1 tablespoon (15 ml) of oil, basil, parsley, chives, oregano and salt. Use a silicone spoonula to fold everything together. Mix until combined.

Preheat the oven to 350°F (175°C, or gas mark 4). Place a baking dish on top of a half sheet pan.

Ladle some red sauce on the bottom of the baking dish and spread it around. Spoon about 1 tablespoonful (16 g) of the ricotta mixture into each shell. Place them close together in the baking dish. Dollop the remaining sauce in between and on top of the shells, without completely covering them.

In a small mixing bowl, combine the breadcrumbs, Parmesan and remaining ½ tablespoon (8 ml) of oil, working it all together until the oil is completely incorporated into the breadcrumbs and Parmesan. Sprinkle on top of the shells.

Cover with foil and bake for 45 minutes. Uncover and cook for another 15 minutes, until the edges of the shells look crispy and the sauce is bubbling.

Let stand for at least 10 minutes to cool slightly before serving.

Tofu Franchaise

Serves 4

Franchaise is an old-school dish that is all about the lemon-butter-wine sauce. Yes, sauce again! I loved Franchaise, but when I learned about how veal calves were raised for food, I banned it from my house. My mother obliged, and that was the end of Franchaise for me. Until now! In this preparation, tofu is the star ingredient. It is cooked in one pan while the sauce is cooked in another. When everything is ready, the tofu is plated, the sauce is poured over top and the platter is sprinkled with fresh parsley. Just like the old days, minus the veal.

¼ cup (24 g) chickpea flour

A pinch of salt and a dash of pepper

1 (15-oz [425-g]) package extra firm tofu, pressed for 10 minutes, cut into 8 triangles

2 tbsp (30 ml) good olive oil

1 lemon, cut into thin slices

½ cup (120 ml) vegan white wine

¼ cup (60 ml) water

2 tbsp (28 g) vegan butter (page 166)

2 tbsp (30 ml) freshly squeezed lemon juice

2 tbsp (8 g) chopped fresh parsley

Season the chickpea flour with salt and pepper. Dredge the tofu in the chickpea flour, coating both sides.

Heat a cast-iron or nonstick skillet over medium heat. Add the oil. When it is shimmering, gently lay the tofu slices onto the pan. Cook for 3 minutes on each side, until lightly browned.

At the same time, caramelize the lemon slices in a small, dry cast-iron or nonstick pan over medium heat. Cook for 3 minutes without moving the lemons until the first side is brown and soft. Use tongs to gently flip the slices over. Cook for another minute.

In a small pot, add the wine, water, butter and lemon juice. Bring to a boil, and reduce to a simmer. Cook for 5 minutes, until the sauce has reduced.

To assemble, arrange the tofu on a platter and top with the caramelized lemons. Pour the sauce over the tofu and lemons, and sprinkle with parsley. Serve immediately.

Paella Verduras

Serves 4

Paella is a dish that originated in Spain, and what makes it special is saffron, once known as the most expensive spice in the world. It's quite possibly my all-time favorite ingredient. Not only does it add flavor, but it colors the rice bright yellow. It's easy to make this classic dish into a vegan pot of deliciousness by using fresh vegetables, briny olives and capers, and frozen peas. Make it any time of the year, for any occasion.

Be sure to use your widest, shallowest pan to make this dish, one with lots of surface area. It's traditional for paella, as it allows the rice and vegetables to cook evenly. Because the rice is so close to the heat, the bottom tends to caramelize, forming a crusty layer called *socarrat*. It is crispy and delicious and probably the best part of the dish!

Paella Verduras

3 cups (720 ml) water
1 tsp crushed saffron
1 tbsp (15 ml) good olive oil
1 white onion, diced
1 red bell pepper, diced
2 cloves garlic, pressed
1 tsp Sazón seasoning
Pinch of salt
2 tbsp (32 g) tomato paste
1½ cups (300 g) uncooked Arborio rice
1 cup (110 g) green beans, trimmed and cut into 1-inch (2.5-cm) pieces
½ cup (64 g) green olives, pitted and cut in half
2 tbsp (18 g) capers, drained
Dash of pepper
¼ cup (34 g) frozen green peas

Toppings
Lemon wedges
Chopped fresh parsley

To steep the saffron, bring the water to a boil. Take the water off the heat, add the saffron and let it steep until ready to use. Set aside.

Heat a paella pan or big shallow pot that has a cover over medium heat. Add the oil. When it is shimmering, add the onion, bell pepper, garlic, Sazón and salt. Sauté until the onion is translucent and the pepper is softening, about 8 minutes. Add the tomato paste and use a wooden spoon to mix it into the vegetables, cooking it for 3 to 4 minutes.

Add the rice and stir around to coat with the tomato paste, toasting it for 1 to 2 minutes. Add the green beans, olives and capers. Stir around. Season with pepper.

Add the saffron-infused water, raise the heat and bring to a boil. Reduce the heat and cover. Simmer gently without stirring the rice for 10 minutes, or until all of the liquid is absorbed and the rice is al dente. Sprinkle with the green peas during the last few minutes of cooking.

Take the pan off the heat and let stand, covered, for 10 minutes.

When ready to serve, fluff up the paella with a fork. Decorate with lemon wedges and sprinkle with parsley. Serve out of the pan.

Deep-Dish Spinach Phyllo Pie

Makes 8 big slices, using a 1.7-quart (1.6-L) pie dish

When I was growing up, we went out for dinner every Wednesday night to a local family-owned coffee shop in town that was famous for its spinach pie. They served it out of a gigantic sheet pan and each square was at least 2 inches (5 cm) thick. Of course, I had to re-create it when I became vegan and, even though it takes a little bit of work, the end result is totally worth it. It's so good, I have been known to eat it cold standing at my kitchen counter.

This recipe calls for two pounds (907 g) of fresh baby spinach, which looks like a lot but wilts down significantly. It also calls for all of the alliums—onions, garlic, scallions, shallots, leeks and chives—because they each add their own flavor, lots of dill, mint and parsley for herby freshness, artichoke hearts for tang and almond feta for texture.

To make this pie happen, be sure to bake the almond feta ahead of time and thaw your phyllo dough as per the package instructions. Then, organize your pie-making plan accordingly.

---

2 lbs (907 g) fresh baby spinach

2 tbsp (30 ml) good olive oil, plus more for the phyllo

1 onion, diced

3 cloves garlic, pressed

1 leek, cleaned and sliced into half-moons

6 scallions, thinly sliced

3 shallots, thinly sliced

1 oz (28 g) chives, thinly sliced

A few big pinches of salt

½ cup (32 g) fresh chopped dill

3 tbsp (18 g) fresh chopped mint

3 tbsp (11 g) fresh chopped parsley

1 (14-oz [397-g]) can artichoke hearts, drained and chopped

1 tbsp (15 ml) freshly squeezed lemon juice

1 recipe Almond Feta (page 50)

1 (16-oz [454-g]) box vegan phyllo, thawed

To prepare the spinach, heat a big pot over medium-low heat. Add the spinach, as big a bunch as you can at one time. Cover it and let it steam down for a minute or so. Then, go in with tongs and toss it around to help it wilt. Add the rest of the spinach and toss until it is completely wilted. Turn the heat off.

Set a strainer over a big bowl. Use tongs to lift the spinach out of the pot, squeezing as you go, leaving any excess water in the pot. Add the spinach to the strainer, pressing it against the sides to release the spinach liquid. Leave the spinach in the strainer and let any excess water drain out while you prepare the rest of the filling.

Clean out the pot and put it back on the stove over medium-low heat. Add the oil and when it is shimmering, add the onion, garlic, leek, scallions, shallots and chives. Season with salt and cook slowly, over medium-low heat, until they are fragrant and translucent, 10 to 12 minutes.

Add the dill, mint, parsley, artichoke hearts and lemon juice. Mix together very well. Drop the spinach onto a cutting board, and run your knife through for a rough chop. Add the spinach a little at a time, and mix it into the alliums and herbs, until everything is completely combined. Crumble the feta over the mixture, and mix gently to incorporate it into the spinach mixture.

(Continued)

Preheat the oven to 400°F (200°C, or gas mark 6). Brush the bottom and sides of your pie dish with oil. Pour more oil in a little bowl.

Roll out the phyllo dough. Use a pizza cutter to cut it in half, to approximate the size of the pie dish. Cover it with a kitchen towel to prevent it from drying out as you work.

Lay a piece of phyllo over the pie dish. Press it down into the bottom of the pie dish and let the ends hang over the sides. Brush with oil. Lay another sheet into the pie dish in the other direction so now the phyllo covers the entire dish. Brush again with oil. Repeat 7 more times, for a total of 9 layers, pressing the phyllo down and to the sides as you brush with oil. Whatever phyllo is sticking out will end up as part of the top layer of the crust.

Transfer the spinach mixture into the phyllo, spread it out and press it down. Take a piece of phyllo and lay it on top of the spinach mixture. Gently press it down and brush with oil. Take another piece and layer it across the spinach, in the other direction, so the spinach is covered. Brush again with oil. Repeat 7 more times, for a total of 9 layers. Fold the excess phyllo down over the center and brush with oil, to seal the deal. The phyllo on the edges may be a little dry but that's okay, it will still look pretty and taste great.

Bake for 30 to 35 minutes, or until the top is brown and crispy. Transfer the pie dish to a cooling rack and let stand for at least 20 minutes. Use a serrated knife to cut into the pie, being sure to go all the way through the bottom crust and cut 8 big slices. Use a small spatula to help you lift the pie slices out of the pie dish.

This pie is even better the next day because the spinach has time to settle. Make it, cover it in foil, store it in the refrigerator and then reheat it in a 350°F (175°C, or gas mark 4) oven for 30 to 35 minutes, or until heated through.

NOTE:

You can find vegan phyllo in the freezer section of your local grocery store. I like The Fillo Factory brand which comes in 1-pound (454-g) boxes of about 18, 13 x 18–inch (33 x 46–cm) sheets. If yours is a different size, don't worry, just use enough to fill out your pie dish. Whatever you don't use, you can refreeze.

Sheet-Pan Portobello Fajitas

with Guacamole and Sour Cream

Serves 4

Fajitas are a staple of Tex-Mex cuisine—meat served with sautéed vegetables, flavorful spices, warm tortillas and delicious toppings. To make it vegan, leave out the meat and add meaty portobello mushrooms instead, for a hearty vegetable-centric variation. In this preparation, I take a shortcut, using a sheet pan, to make this an easy-to-clean-up meal. Everything is tossed in classic fajita seasonings and roasted until charred and tender. Served with warm tortillas, guacamole and sour cream, it's a big, satisfying, flavorful meal.

Fajitas

2 portobello mushrooms, stems and gills removed, sliced into strips

½ onion, thinly sliced into half-moons

½ red bell pepper, thinly sliced

½ orange bell pepper, thinly sliced

½ yellow bell pepper, thinly sliced

2 tbsp (30 ml) sunflower oil

2 tsp (5 g) chili powder

½ tsp cumin

¼ tsp paprika

¼ tsp garlic powder

¼ tsp onion powder

Pinch of salt

Preheat the oven to 400°F (200°C, or gas mark 6). Line a half sheet pan with parchment paper.

Add the mushrooms, onion and bell peppers to the sheet pan. Drizzle with the oil and toss to coat. In a small bowl, combine the chili powder, cumin, paprika, garlic powder, onion powder and salt. Sprinkle the spices over the vegetable mixture and toss again to coat. Arrange in a single layer and bake for 30 minutes, until the vegetables start to soften and brown.

To warm the tortillas, wrap them in foil and place in the oven for the last 10 minutes of the vegetable cooking time or heat them on a dry cast-iron skillet.

(Continued)

Guacamole

1 avocado, peeled and pitted

2 tbsp (20 g) finely diced red onion

1 tbsp (15 ml) freshly squeezed lime juice

2 tsp (scant 1 g) chopped fresh cilantro

2 tsp (4 g) chopped fresh mint

Big pinch of salt

To Serve

Flour tortillas

Sour cream (page 85)

Lime wedges

To make the guacamole, add the avocado to a small mixing bowl and mash with a fork. Add the onion, lime juice, cilantro, mint and salt. Mix together. Taste the guacamole and add more of any of the ingredients until it is to your liking.

Serve with tortillas, guacamole, sour cream and lime wedges.

NOTE:

I love a good bowl of guacamole—but sometimes there just isn't enough onion, lime juice or salt. It all depends on the avocado, the juiciness of the lime and how many margaritas I've had. So, I always start with the measurements listed and go from there.

Creamy Risotto

with Shredded Zucchini and Basil Kale Pesto

Serves 4

Doesn't risotto seem like a fancy dish that would be hard to make at home? Well, it's not! It's actually easy, no more than half an hour from start to finish. Once you learn the process, the possibilities are endless. First, you sauté some aromatics, then you toast Arborio rice and then you slowly add warm liquid, a little at a time, until it is fully absorbed. You know it's done when the rice is al dente and the risotto is creamy. Are you wondering how it can possibly get creamy without any dairy? That slow cooking process coaxes the starches out of the rice. It becomes creamy all by itself, plus a little vegan butter doesn't hurt. It's a blank canvas to which you can add anything you want. In this preparation, shredded zucchini adds a little earthiness and herby pesto, also made without cheese, adds brightness. It's like that old saying, teach a cook to make risotto and feed them for a lifetime!

Risotto

1 big zucchini, shredded
1 tsp salt, plus a pinch
4 cups (960 ml) water
1 tbsp (15 ml) good olive oil
6 shallots, thinly sliced
2 cloves garlic, pressed
1 cup (200 g) uncooked Arborio rice
1 cup (240 ml) vegan white wine
1 tbsp (14 g) vegan butter (page 166)
1 tsp fresh lemon zest

To prepare the zucchini, add the zucchini into a fine-mesh strainer over a bowl. Sprinkle with a teaspoon of salt and mix around with a fork. Let stand to drain. Use the fork to press the zucchini against the strainer to release as much water as possible. Set aside.

Bring the water to a boil. Turn the heat to low to keep the water warm.

Heat a pot over medium-low heat. Add the oil. When it is shimmering, add the shallots, garlic and salt. Sauté until the shallots become translucent, about 7 minutes.

Add the rice and toss around to coat with oil. The grains will start to turn translucent. Add the wine, stir occasionally and cook until the wine is absorbed, 6 to 7 minutes.

Add a ladle or two of water to the rice. Cook until the water is absorbed, stirring occasionally. Add another ladle of water, stir occasionally and cook until absorbed. Keep going until the risotto is creamy and al dente. You may not use all of the water.

(Continued)

Basil Kale Pesto

½ cup (about 14 g) packed fresh basil leaves

½ cup (34 g) packed baby kale

1 clove garlic

2 tbsp (17 g) raw pine nuts

½ tbsp (9 g) mellow white miso

2 tbsp (30 ml) good olive oil

¼ tsp salt

To make the pesto, add the basil, baby kale, garlic, pine nuts, miso, oil and salt to the food processor. Process until the pesto is smooth.

To finish the risotto, add the drained zucchini and butter. Stir them into the risotto, cover, and let stand for 2 minutes.

Ladle the risotto into wide shallow bowls. Top with lemon zest and a dollop of pesto.

NOTE:

Pesto is easy to veganize by leaving out the Parmesan cheese and adding in miso for that salty, fermented flavor. It's super versatile so play around with the ingredients. Go all basil or substitute the kale with arugula or spinach. And, while pine nuts are traditional, walnuts, pecans and pistachios are all delicious. You probably won't use all of the pesto for this dish; store the rest in the freezer, covered with a layer of olive oil, and use it whenever. It is really good in a Scrambled Tofu (page 14), as a layer inside of lasagna (page 127) or as a topping on stuffed shells (page 112).

Vegetable Lasagna

Serves 8 to 12

Lasagna is the perfect centerpiece for any holiday get together, party or potluck. It's all about the layers—noodles, sauce, cheese, noodles, sauce, cheese. In this version, the noodles are layered with a vegetable-heavy sauce and creamy ricotta. The whole thing is topped off with fresh tomatoes and basil. Once you get the layering down, have fun and get creative. Lasagna is one of those dishes that will be delicious no matter what. Try it with Lentil Bolognese (page 86), Basil Kale Pesto (page 126) or steamed greens. Just layer them in there somewhere for the perfect bite.

Vegetable Sauce

2 tbsp (30 ml) good olive oil
½ medium onion, diced small
2 big cloves garlic, pressed
A few pinches of salt
½ red bell pepper, diced small
½ orange bell pepper, diced small
½ yellow bell pepper, diced small
1 medium zucchini, diced small
½ medium eggplant, diced small
1 tbsp fresh thyme
1 (4.5-oz [127-g]) tube of tomato paste
1 (28-oz [794-g]) can crushed tomatoes
1 cup (240 ml) water

To make the sauce, heat a heavy bottomed pot over low heat. Add the oil. When it is shimmering, add the onion. When the onion is translucent, about 7 minutes, add the garlic and a pinch of salt. Cook for a minute. Add the bell peppers, zucchini, eggplant, thyme and another pinch of salt. Cover and cook for 10 minutes, until the vegetables have softened. Add the tomato paste and use a wooden spoon to mix it into the vegetables, cooking it for 3 to 4 minutes.

Add the can of tomatoes to the pot. Add the water to the can and swirl it around so that you get the rest of whatever is left. Pour it into the pot and stir around. Season with a final pinch of salt. Bring up to a nice simmer and cook uncovered for 30 minutes, stirring occasionally, until the sauce has thickened.

(Continued)

Vegetable Lasagna (Continued)

Lasagna

4 tbsp (60 ml) good olive oil, divided

1 (16-oz [454-g]) box uncooked lasagna noodles

2 cups (456 g) Almond Ricotta (page 169)

1 cup (240 ml) cashew milk (page 174)

Pinch of salt

½ cup (120 ml) Cashew Cream (page 165)

16 slices of vine-ripened tomatoes

3 tbsp (24 g) Seasoned Breadcrumbs (page 178)

1 tbsp (7 g) Almond Parmesan (page 177)

A few leaves of basil, cut into chiffonade

To make the lasagna noodles, bring a large pot of salted water with 1 tablespoon (15 ml) of oil to a boil. Have a half sheet pan at the ready. Cook the lasagna noodles for 5 minutes. Drain the noodles into a colander and run them under cold water, swooshing the noodles around so they don't stick to each other. Quickly lift them out and lay them onto the sheet pan. It's okay if they overlap.

To prepare the cheese, add the ricotta, cashew milk, 2 tablespoons (30 ml) of oil and salt to a small mixing bowl. Use a silicone spoonula to fold everything together. Mix until combined.

To make the lasagna, preheat the oven to 350°F (175°C, or gas mark 4). Place your baking dish on a half sheet pan.

Ladle a bit of sauce on the bottom of the baking dish, just to coat it. Add a layer of lasagna noodles on top of the sauce, overlapping them slightly, if necessary. Dollop ricotta over the noodles and spread it out. Ladle sauce over the cheese and spread it out to cover the cheese. Add another layer of noodles, overlapping them slightly, and layer with cheese and sauce. Continue layering, until you use everything up, ending with sauce. Drizzle the top layer of sauce with cashew cream. Decorate the top of the lasagna with sliced tomatoes, overlapping them as you go.

In a small mixing bowl, combine the breadcrumbs, Parmesan, and 1 tablespoon (15 ml) of oil, working it all together until the oil is completely incorporated into the breadcrumbs and Parmesan. Sprinkle on top of the lasagna.

Cover with foil and bake for 45 minutes. Uncover and cook for another 15 minutes, until the tomatoes are soft and wilted and the edges of the pasta look crispy.

Let stand for at least 20 minutes to cool slightly and set before slicing. Garnish with the basil and serve.

DESSERTS

Who needs breakfast, lunch and dinner when there's dessert?
Here, classics such as vanilla cake, chocolate chip cookies, blueberry
pie and pecan pie get a vegan makeover. Any one of these treats will
be a big hit at a party, your office, a potluck or your kid's classroom!

Vanilla Cupcakes

with Vanilla Bean Buttercream Frosting

Makes 12

Your arsenal of vegan desserts starts right here. Vanilla doesn't mean ordinary or basic. In the case of these cupcakes, it means light, fluffy and magically delicious. Made without animal products and virtually allergen-free, these little beauties are easy to make and great for a kid's birthday party or really any celebration for that matter.

In my world, the only thing better than a delicious cupcake, is the frosting on top. Can you make lusciously sweet vegan buttercream? Yes . . . with vegan butter and shortening. Just like with its dairy counterpart, the key to perfect buttercream is to ensure that all of the ingredients are the same temperature. That way, the buttercream won't break. Frost your cupcakes in any design you like, and decorate them with some fun and colorful sprinkles!

Vanilla Cupcakes

1½ cups (188 g) all-purpose flour
1 tsp baking soda
½ tsp salt
1 cup (200 g) vegan cane sugar
1 cup (240 ml) cold water
6 tbsp (90 ml) sunflower oil
1 tbsp (15 ml) apple cider vinegar
1 tsp vanilla extract

To make the cupcakes, preheat the oven to 350°F (175°C, or gas mark 4). Place cupcake liners in each cupcake well.

Add the flour, baking soda and salt into a big mixing bowl. Mix together well. Add the sugar, water, oil, vinegar and vanilla. Mix, using a hand mixer on low, until the batter is smooth.

Add ¼ cup (60 ml) of batter to each cupcake liner. If there is any excess batter, distribute it evenly.

Bake for 25 to 30 minutes, or until a tester comes out clean. When cool enough to touch, lift the cupcakes out of the cupcake pan and place them on a cooling rack. Cool completely before frosting.

(Continued)

Vanilla Bean Buttercream Frosting

¼ cup (48 g) vegan butter (page 166), room temperature

¼ cup (48 g) vegan shortening

2½ cups (300 g) vegan powdered sugar, divided

¼ cup (60 ml) water, room temperature

1 tsp vanilla extract

½ tsp ground vanilla beans

Pinch of salt

To make the frosting, place the butter and shortening in a big mixing bowl. Use a hand mixer to whip them together until nice and creamy. Add about 1 cup (120 g) of powdered sugar and, with the mixer on low, mix to incorporate. Add the rest of the sugar, along with the water, vanilla, vanilla beans and salt. Starting with the mixer on low, continue mixing until the frosting is smooth and fluffy, about 3 minutes.

Use an offset spatula or piping bag to frost the cupcakes.

NOTE:

Be sure to look for sugar that is labeled "suitable for vegans." Many commercial brands process their sugar using bone char.

VARIATIONS:

This batter can also be used to make other shapes and sizes. Here are the approximate yields and baking times:

1 (9-inch [23-cm]) layer cake, 45 minutes

6 mini Bundt cakes, 25 minutes

30 mini cupcakes, 15 minutes

Recipe doubled for 1 big cake, 60 minutes

Buttermilk Biscuit Strawberry Shortcakes

with Lemon Vanilla Cream

Makes 4

Is there anything better than light and fluffy biscuits right out of the oven? I really don't think so! I love them so much that I became obsessed with creating an easy recipe for drop-style biscuits. Once I perfected them, I immediately thought they would be perfect filled with juicy macerated strawberries for a fun take on strawberry shortcakes. Topped with fresh lemon vanilla cream, they really are out of this world. If you are feeling extra fancy, kick it up a notch and add a drizzle of balsamic reduction (page 63) and a little extra zest over the top.

Macerated Strawberries
½ lb (226 g) fresh strawberries, hulled and sliced
1 tbsp (15 g) vegan cane sugar

Buttermilk Biscuits
½ cup (120 ml) unsweetened soy milk
½ tbsp (8 ml) apple cider vinegar
1 cup (125 g) all-purpose flour
1 tsp baking powder
1 tsp baking soda
¼ tsp salt
6 tbsp (90 ml) sunflower oil

To macerate the strawberries, add them to a small bowl. Sprinkle with sugar and mix together. Let stand at room temperature for 30 minutes, until the strawberries soften and release their juices.

To make the buttermilk, pour the milk into a measuring cup. Add the vinegar, and use a fork to beat it together. Let stand for 5 minutes to acidulate. It will be lumpy.

Preheat the oven to 475°F (240°C, or gas mark 9). Line a quarter sheet pan with parchment paper.

Whisk together the flour, baking powder, baking soda and salt.

Add the oil to a small mixing bowl. Add the buttermilk and whisk them together.

Pour the wet ingredients into the dry ingredients. Mix well until a nice ball of dough forms.

Using a 4-tablespoon (60-ml) scooper or a ¼-cup (60-ml) measuring cup, drop scoops of batter about 1 inch (2.5-cm) apart on the prepared sheet pan.

(Continued)

Buttermilk Biscuit Strawberry Shortcakes with Lemon Vanilla Cream (Continued)

Lemon Vanilla Cream

½ cup (120 ml) Cashew Cream (page 165)

1 tbsp (15 ml) golden maple syrup

1 tbsp (6 g) fresh lemon zest

1 tsp vanilla extract

¼ tsp ground vanilla beans

Bake until the tops are starting to turn golden brown, 11 to 13 minutes. Let the biscuits cool.

To make the lemon vanilla cream, mix the cashew cream, maple syrup, lemon zest, vanilla and vanilla beans together.

To assemble the strawberry shortcakes, place the biscuit bottom on a serving dish. Layer with macerated strawberries and lemon vanilla cream. Place the top of the biscuit askew and serve.

NOTE:

Just because these biscuits are in the dessert chapter, doesn't mean you can't eat them with dinner. Just don't fill them up with strawberries! Keep them plain, or make them savory by adding a variety of herbs such as chives, lemon thyme and parsley.

Chocolate Chip Cookies

Makes 16

There is nothing more delicious than a crispy-on-the-outside-chewy-on-the-inside chocolate chip cookie. I am sure everyone's family has their own recipe, but this is the veganized version of my mom's, which she probably got off the back of the bag of chocolate chips. And because there are no eggs in this recipe, you can eat the cookie dough right out of the bowl. Bonus!

These cookies spread a lot while baking, so leave a lot of room between them. If you have more than one sheet pan, make them simultaneously. Otherwise, make five or six cookies at a time.

1½ cups (188 g) all-purpose flour

½ cup (120 g) vegan mini semisweet chocolate chips `

½ tsp baking soda

½ tsp baking powder

½ tsp salt

6 tbsp (90 ml) aquafaba, room temperature

1 cup (200 g) vegan cane sugar

¼ cup (55 g) packed vegan brown sugar

½ cup (120 ml) sunflower oil

1 tsp vanilla extract

Preheat the oven to 350°F (175°C, or gas mark 4). Line three half sheet pans with parchment paper.

Mix the flour, chocolate chips, baking soda, baking powder and salt in a big bowl.

In a separate medium-sized mixing bowl, whisk the aquafaba until it becomes foamy and white. Add the cane sugar, brown sugar, oil and vanilla. Whisk to combine.

Pour the wet ingredients into the dry ingredients. Mix with a silicone spoonula or wooden spoon until it fully comes together into a dough.

Using a 3-tablespoon (45-ml) scooper, scoop out the dough, pressing it on the side of the bowl to pack it well. Drop the cookie dough onto the sheet pan, leaving a lot of space in between.

Bake for 13 to 15 minutes until the edges are dry and the centers are just set. Remove the sheet pans from the oven, and use a thin spatula to transfer the cookies onto a cooling rack. Cool completely.

NOTE:

To keep brown sugar from hardening up, place a piece of bread in the bag and seal tightly.

Chocolate Chocolate-Chip Mini Bundt Cakes

Makes 6, using 6 (4 x 1.75") Bundt pans

When I was a kid, my mother served a chocolate Bundt cake for every single party we ever had. It was so pretty because of the design built right into the pan. She followed a recipe written on a pink piece of paper that called for a box of cake mix, instant chocolate pudding mix, eggs and chocolate chips. She always served it with a dusting of powdered sugar on top. It was fudgy, rich and full of artificial ingredients. Those days are long gone and now this is our go-to, from scratch, fudgy, rich chocolate cake formula.

Whenever I make these cakes for a special occasion, I serve them with chocolate glaze on three of them and, to honor my childhood dessert, a dusting of powdered sugar on the other three. That way everyone gets to choose their favorite. You can go all glaze or all powdered sugar—whatever works for you!

Chocolate Bundts

1½ cups (188 g) all-purpose flour

¼ cup (22 g) cocoa powder

1 tsp baking soda

½ tsp salt

1 cup (200 g) vegan cane sugar

1 cup (240 ml) cold water

6 tbsp (90 ml) sunflower oil, plus extra for brushing

1 tbsp (15 ml) apple cider vinegar

1 tsp vanilla extract

½ cup (120 g) vegan mini semisweet chocolate chips

To make the chocolate Bundts, preheat the oven to 350°F (175°C, or gas mark 4). Lightly brush the Bundt wells with oil.

Add the flour, cocoa powder, baking soda and salt into a big mixing bowl. Mix together very well, making sure there are no clumps. Add the sugar, water, oil, vinegar and vanilla. Mix, using a hand mixer on low, until the batter is smooth. Add the chocolate chips and use a wooden spoon to incorporate.

Add ½ cup (120 ml) of batter to each Bundt well. If there is any excess batter, distribute it evenly.

Bake for 25 to 30 minutes or until a tester comes out clean. Be sure you hit the cake and not a chip. Immediately run an offset spatula around the edges of the Bundts.

When the Bundts have significantly cooled, run the offset spatula around the edges again, and gently use it to work the Bundts out of the pan. Place them on a cooling rack, top side down, pretty Bundt side up. Cool completely.

(Continued)

Wait, That's Vegan?!

Chocolate Glaze
½ cup (60 g) vegan powdered sugar
1 tbsp (5 g) cocoa powder
1 tbsp plus ½ tsp (18 ml) water
¼ tsp vanilla extract
Pinch of salt

Topping
Powdered sugar

To make the glaze, add the powdered sugar, cocoa powder, water, vanilla and salt to a small mixing bowl. Use a silicone spoonula to mix together until smooth.

To decorate, dip the tops of three of the Bundts into the glaze, pressing them and gently angling them around to ensure the whole top is covered. Place them back on the cooling rack to drip dry.

Add a little powdered sugar into a fine-mesh strainer. Hold it over each of the remaining three Bundts and hit the edge of the strainer with your palm for a light dusting of sugar.

VARIATIONS:

This batter can also be used to make other shapes and sizes. Here are the approximate yields and baking times:

1 (9-inch [23-cm]) layer cake, 45 minutes

1 dozen cupcakes, 25 minutes

30 mini cupcakes, 15 minutes

Recipe doubled for 1 big cake, 60 minutes

Blueberry Hand Pies

Makes 6

Along with the rest of the desserts in this chapter, pie brings back all kinds of fun food memories for me, particularly, blueberry pie. It is my sister's favorite, and I love nothing more than making her something she loves to eat. Pie is pretty easy to veganize because it's really all about the crust. The Little Pie Crust bakes up buttery and crispy—without any butter. Instead of a whole pie, I am sticking with my mini dessert theme and making individual hand pies. They are way cuter and more fun to eat. Plus, they are so much easier to wrap up for delivery!

Filling
½ cup (74 g) fresh blueberries
1 tsp fresh lemon zest
1 tsp freshly squeezed lemon juice
1 tsp all-purpose flour
1 tsp coconut sugar
Pinch of salt

Hand Pie Dough
1 recipe The Little Pie Crust (page 181)

Preheat the oven to 400°F (200°C, or gas mark 6). Line a half sheet pan with parchment paper.

To prepare the blueberries, place them into a small mixing bowl and sprinkle with lemon zest and juice, flour, sugar and salt. Use a silicone spoonula to gently coat the blueberries. A light slurry will form. Set aside.

Roll out the dough to about 12 inches (30 cm) around and ⅛-inch (3-mm) thick. Use a 3⅜-inch (8.5-cm) pastry cutter to cut 6 circles for the bottoms. Lay them on the center of the sheet pan, with some space in between.

There should still be plenty of dough available to cut. Use a 3½-inch (9-cm) pastry cutter to cut as many circles as you can for the tops. Place them on the sheet pan, but off to the side.

When you have run out of dough, but still need a few more circles, gather up the dough scraps, reform it into a ball and roll it out again. Cut the remaining circles and place to the side of the sheet pan.

Carefully spoon about 1 tablespoon (about 9 g) of blueberries onto the bottom circles, leaving a 1½-inch (3.5-cm) border, spreading them out evenly. Spoon any extra slurry over the top of the blueberries.

Lay the top dough circles right over the top of the blueberries, matching the edges. Use the tines of a fork to press the edge of the top piece of dough into the edge of the bottom pieces. Use a paring knife to cut a little "x" on the top of each pie.

(Continued)

Glaze

1 tbsp (20 g) thick apricot preserves

2 tbsp (30 ml) water

To make the glaze, whisk the apricot preserves with the water, and lightly brush over the pies.

Bake for 25 to 30 minutes, until the crust is golden brown. Serve warm or at room temperature.

Coconut White Chocolate Crème Brûlée

Makes 6, using 6 (3-oz [85-ml] ramekins)

My son is a big fan of the crispy burnt sugar tops of these crème brûlées. Can you blame him? It is tasty, but it gets even better when it's cracked open to reveal the custard inside. Yes, even custard can be made vegan, with coconut milk and cashew cream. These little bowls of goodness are the epitome of an impressive and elegant dessert. Serve them at a dinner party or even on a random weeknight!

This recipe is easy but a little specific, so be prepared. You need a kitchen scale to measure the cacao butter. You also need ramekins to serve it in and a torch to burn the sugar topping. With that said, this still ranks up there with the easiest desserts to make. It all happens on the stovetop; no baking required.

1 (13.5-oz [400-ml]) can classic unsweetened coconut milk

¼ cup (60 ml) Cashew Cream (page 165)

¼ cup (50 g) vegan cane sugar, plus more for the brûlée

2 tbsp (16 g) arrowroot starch/flour

2 tsp (10 ml) vanilla extract

½ oz (14 g) cacao butter

Tiny pinch of salt

Set your ramekins on a quarter sheet pan and make room in the refrigerator.

Combine the coconut milk, cashew cream, sugar, arrowroot, vanilla, cacao butter and salt in a small pot. Whisk together over medium heat until the cacao butter is melted, about 5 minutes; the mixture will start to boil, pull away from the sides of the pot and coat the whisk. Pour into your ramekins, cover and chill for at least 2 hours, until set.

Evenly sprinkle the top of each ramekin with sugar. Torch and burn the sugar, until it is dark and crispy.

Oatmeal Raisin Cookies

Makes 30 cookies

Oatmeal raisin cookies are healthy right? Oats and raisins make it so. Well not really, there is lots of sugar for sweetness baked into these babies. Funny, though, I never even liked oatmeal raisin cookies until I made them myself! These cook up like brittle or lace cookies. With just a hint of cinnamon, and magical aquafaba as the egg replacer, these little gems may just become your new favorite cookie for teatime or an afternoon snack.

You will need more than two sheet pans to bake all of these cookies. Each half sheet pan can accommodate 12 cookies, so prepare accordingly.

1½ cups (135 g) old-fashioned oats

1 cup (145 g) raisins

½ cup (63 g) all-purpose flour

½ tsp baking soda

½ tsp baking powder

½ tsp salt

¼ tsp cinnamon

¼ cup (60 ml) aquafaba, room temperature

1 cup (200 g) vegan cane sugar

½ cup (120 ml) sunflower oil

1 tsp vanilla extract

Preheat the oven to 350°F (175°C, or gas mark 4). Line two half sheet pans with parchment paper.

Mix the oats, raisins, flour, baking soda, baking powder, salt and cinnamon into a big mixing bowl.

In a separate medium mixing bowl, whisk the aquafaba until it becomes foamy and white. Add the sugar, oil and vanilla. Whisk to combine.

Pour the wet ingredients into the dry ingredients. Mix with a silicone spoonula or wooden spoon until it fully comes together.

Using a 1-tablespoon (15-ml) scooper, scoop out the dough, pressing it on the side of the bowl to pack it well. Drop the cookie dough onto the sheet pan, leaving a bit of space in between. Press the tops of the cookies down a little bit.

Bake for 18 to 20 minutes, until the cookies are brown and crispy. Remove the sheet pans from the oven, and let the cookies cool on the pans. They will continue to harden up as they cool.

Crackly Brownies

Makes 16 brownies

When I was telling a friend about the dessert chapter of this book, she assumed there was going to be a brownie recipe in it, because everyone needs a good brownie recipe. I told her that I tried everything over the years, without success, using all kinds of egg replacers and other ingredients. The only thing I didn't try was melting chocolate into the batter. Um, hello? Why not? So, I went into full recipe development mode and, with a little tinkering and a lot of melted chocolate, I came up with this recipe. These little squares hit every mark: fudgy, chewy and crackly. You need to make these right now.

1 cup (240 g) vegan mini semisweet chocolate chips

1 cup (125 g) all-purpose flour

1 tsp baking powder

½ tsp salt

¼ cup (60 ml) aquafaba, room temperature

1 cup (220 g) packed vegan brown sugar

3 tbsp (45 ml) sunflower oil

1 tsp vanilla extract

Preheat the oven to 350°F (175°C, or gas mark 4). Line a 8 x 8–inch (20 x 20–cm) brownie pan with parchment paper.

Place the chocolate chips in a double boiler or in a heatproof bowl over a pot of boiling water. Mix with a silicone spoonula and melt until smooth. Take the chocolate off the heat and set aside.

Add the flour, baking powder and salt into a big mixing bowl. Mix together well.

In a separate medium mixing bowl, whisk the aquafaba until it becomes foamy and white. Add the brown sugar, oil and vanilla. Whisk to combine. Fold in the melted chocolate chips.

Pour the wet ingredients into the dry ingredients. Mix until the batter comes together. It will be thick. Turn the batter out into the brownie pan and press it to the edges; even it out, using a silicone spoonula, a small measuring cup, or a glass.

Bake for 20 to 25 minutes, or until a tester comes out clean. Let the brownies cool in the pan for 10 minutes. Lift the brownies out by the parchment, place them on a cooling rack and cool completely before cutting into squares.

NOTE:

Parchment paper can be a little challenging when it comes to lining a small pan. To make it easier to work with, crumple it up, run a little water over it and squeeze it out. It will become soft and pliable. Spread it out, dry it off and use as needed.

Seasonal Fruit Galettes

Makes 8 pieces

Since every season has its own best fruit, you need a galette for each one. In the fall, I like to go apple picking and bake up whatever we pick. Any apple works, really, so use your favorite. In the spring, as soon as rhubarb starts to show up at the market, I pop it right into the oven with some fresh strawberries. It is the perfect culinary marriage and, honestly, it's the only thing I know what to make with it! And then when summer rolls around, it's stone fruit season. I go right for the peaches, but nectarines and plums work too. So, pick up the freshest fruits you can find, and get baking!

Galette Dough

1 recipe The Little Pie Crust (page 181)

Apple Filling

2 apples, cored, peeled, and cut into ¼-inch (6-mm) slices

1 tbsp (9 g) coconut sugar

1 tsp all-purpose flour

¼ tsp cinnamon

Pinch of salt

Strawberry-Rhubarb Filling

2 cups (288 g) fresh strawberries, hulled and sliced crosswise

1 stalk fresh rhubarb, thinly sliced, about ½ cup (61 g)

1 tbsp (9 g) coconut sugar

1 tsp all-purpose flour

¼ tsp ground vanilla beans

Pinch of salt

Preheat the oven to 400°F (200°C, or gas mark 6). Line a half sheet pan with parchment paper.

Roll out the dough to about 12 inches (30 cm) around and ⅛-inch (3-mm) thick. Lift it up and flip it over onto the sheet pan.

To make the apple galette, place the apples in a medium mixing bowl. Sprinkle them with coconut sugar, flour, cinnamon and salt. Toss to coat well, until a little slurry forms. Arrange the apples in a circle on the dough, overlapping the apples just slightly, leaving a 1½-inch (3.5-cm) border of dough, working the apples in circles toward the center.

To make the strawberry-rhubarb galette, place the strawberries and rhubarb in a medium mixing bowl. Sprinkle them with coconut sugar, flour, vanilla beans and salt. Toss to coat well, until a little slurry forms. Transfer the strawberry-rhubarb mixture to the dough and spread it out evenly; leave a 1½-inch (3.5-cm) border of dough.

(Continued)

Seasonal Fruit Galettes (Continued)

Peach-Raspberry Filling

4 soft, ripe, baseball-sized peaches, pitted, and cut into ¼-inch (6-mm) slices

1 tbsp (9 g) coconut sugar

1 tsp all-purpose flour

1 tsp fresh lemon zest

1 tsp freshly squeezed lemon juice

Pinch of salt

½ cup (62 g) fresh raspberries

Glaze

2 tbsp (30 ml) water

1 tbsp (20 g) thick apricot preserves

To make the peach-raspberry filling, place the peaches in a medium mixing bowl. Sprinkle with the coconut sugar, flour, lemon zest, lemon juice and salt. Toss to coat well, until a little slurry forms. Transfer the peach mixture to the dough and spread it out evenly; leave a 1½-inch (3.5-cm) border of dough. Arrange the raspberries on top of the peaches.

Fold the edges of the dough over the filling, pleating it as you go around. If it tears, just pinch it back together.

To make the glaze, whisk the water and apricot preserves together. Brush the glaze over the edges and the top of the crust, and on top of the filling.

Bake for 45 to 50 minutes, until the crust is golden brown and the fruit is tender. Let the galettes stand for at least 15 minutes before cutting into them. Serve warm or at room temperature.

Classic New York Cheesecake

with Berry Compote

Serves 8 to 12

If you really want to impress people, make this cheesecake. There are no words to describe how mind-blowingly creamy and delicious it is. No one would guess it is vegan, and it shouldn't matter anyway, when it is this good. This is one of those desserts that will have your guests asking for seconds and thirds. I like to serve it topped with berry compote, but if that's not your jam, nix it and serve it plain.

You have to use good vegan cream cheese for this cake. There are a few brands out there, but like with all packaged ingredients, be sure what you buy is super clean with no unnecessary additives. I use Kite Hill for this recipe.

Crust

2 cups (205 g) graham cracker crumbs, about 15 graham crackers

6 tbsp (90 ml) melted refined coconut oil

¼ cup (55 g) packed vegan brown sugar

Filling

3 (8-oz [226-g]) packages vegan cream cheese, room temperature

1 cup (200 g) vegan cane sugar

1 cup (240 ml) Cashew Cream (page 165), room temperature

2 tbsp (16 g) arrowroot starch/flour

1 tbsp (15 ml) freshly squeezed lemon juice

1 tsp vanilla extract

½ tsp salt

Preheat the oven to 350°F (175°C, or gas mark 4). Line a 9-inch (23-cm) springform pan with a parchment round and place it on a half sheet pan.

To make the crust, add the graham crackers to the food processor and process until fine crumbs form. Add the oil and brown sugar and pulse, scraping down the sides and bottom once or twice, until everything is incorporated.

Turn the crust out into the springform pan and press evenly. Use the bottom of a measuring cup or glass to press and spread it out to the edges.

Bake for 8 minutes. Take out the pan and set aside while making the filling.

To make the filling, add the cream cheese to the bowl of a stand mixer or a big mixing bowl, if using a hand mixer. Turn the mixer to low and work the cream cheese until it's fluffy, scraping down the sides once or twice, about 2 or 3 minutes.

Add the sugar and mix on low until well incorporated. Add in the cashew cream, arrowroot, lemon juice, vanilla and salt. Mix on low for another minute.

Pour the filling into the springform and spread it out evenly. Bake until the cheesecake is set in the center and the edges are just starting to brown, 55 minutes to 1 hour. Take the cheesecake out of the oven and run a paring knife or offset spatula around the edges to separate it from the pan.

(Continued)

Classic New York Cheesecake with Berry Compote (Continued)

Berry Compote

1 cup (150 g) mixed berries, such as blackberries, blueberries and raspberries

1 tbsp (15 g) vegan cane sugar

1 tbsp (15 ml) water

Let the cheesecake sit on the counter and cool completely. Then, cover it and refrigerate overnight to let the cheesecake completely set.

When you are ready to serve, bring the cheesecake up to room temperature. Open the spring and take the ring off the cake.

To make the berry compote, place the berries, sugar and water in a small pot. Cook over medium-low heat. Using a silicone spoonula, stir occasionally, until the berries become soft and juicy, about 5 minutes, breaking them up just a bit. Take the pot off the heat and cool.

Serve the cheesecake slices topped with berry compote.

Chocolate Pudding Parfaits

Makes 4

My favorite after-school snack was, and still is, chocolate pudding. Back then it was a box of My*T*Fine, but when I got older and learned what was in there, I bailed on it pretty quickly. When I learned how to make major substitutions for all kinds of ingredients, I discovered that avocados become super creamy and delicious when whipped up. With a little vegan magic, in the form of cashew milk, plus cacao for the chocolate, maple syrup for the sweetness and maca powder for that malted flavor, boom, we've got chocolate pudding! It is amazing right out of the blender, but it's elevated when layered with vanilla cream and fresh raspberries. It's a "dessert" that could easily be breakfast or a snack.

Chocolate Pudding
1 cup (240 ml) cashew milk (page 174)

1 avocado, peeled and pitted

¼ cup (24 g) raw cacao powder

¼ cup (60 ml) dark maple syrup

1 tbsp (15 g) maca powder

½ tsp ground vanilla beans

Pinch of salt

Vanilla Cream
½ cup (120 ml) Cashew Cream (page 165)

1 tbsp (15 ml) golden maple syrup

1 tsp vanilla extract

¼ tsp ground vanilla beans

Pinch of salt

Parfaits
Fresh raspberries

Cacao nibs

To make the chocolate pudding, add the cashew milk, avocado, raw cacao powder, maple syrup, maca powder, vanilla beans and salt to a blender. Blend until smooth.

To make the vanilla cream, mix the cashew cream, maple syrup, vanilla, vanilla beans and salt together.

To assemble the parfaits, add the chocolate pudding to the bottom of a jar or small bowl. Layer with vanilla cream, then add the raspberries and top with cacao nibs.

If not using immediately, store the pudding and the vanilla cream separately in the refrigerator in sealed containers for up to 3 days.

Pecan Pie Squares

Makes 16 squares

Pecan pie was one of my all-time favorite desserts before I became vegan. I honestly could only eat it once a year, during the holidays, because that gooey filling was so cloyingly sweet that I considered it a treat. I never thought a vegan version was even possible, but I was inspired by a slice of pecan pie I had at Candle Cafe in New York City. It was love at first bite and I got right into the kitchen to start experimenting. Well, here you have it. I found a way to make vegan pecan pie filling, that is as good as any you've ever had—but it's still pretty sweet, so I turned it into cute little squares instead.

---

2 cups (200 g) pecan halves

1 flax egg (1 flax egg = 1 tbsp [7 g] flax meal + 3 tbsp [45 ml] water)

1 recipe The Little Pie Crust (page 181)

1 cup (220 g) packed vegan brown sugar

1 tsp vanilla extract

1 tsp salt

½ cup (120 ml) Cashew Cream (page 165)

½ cup (100 g) vegan cane sugar

1 tbsp (8 g) arrowroot starch/flour

Preheat the oven to 350°F (175°C, or gas mark 4). Have a 8 x 8-inch (20 x 20-cm) brownie pan and a piece of parchment paper at the ready.

To prepare the pecans, line a half sheet pan with parchment paper and arrange the pecans in a single layer. Bake for 10 to 15 minutes, until the pecans have turned a few shades darker. Remove the pan from the oven, leave the oven on and let cool.

To make the flax egg, use a fork to whisk together the flax and water. Set aside for 5 minutes to thicken.

Roll out the dough to as close to 8 x 8 inches (20 x 20 cm) as you can get it, erring on the side of a little bigger. Lay the parchment paper over the top of the dough, flip it over and place it into the brownie pan. Gently press it evenly into the bottom. If there is excess dough, just press it into the bottom. Set aside.

Chop the pecans into small pieces and add them to a big mixing bowl. Add the flax egg, brown sugar, vanilla and salt. Mix very well, fully coating the pecans.

In a small pot, combine the cashew cream, cane sugar and arrowroot. Whisk over medium heat, until thick and bubbly and pulling away from the sides of the pot.

Pour the hot mixture into the pecans and mix very well. Transfer the mixture onto the dough and spread out evenly.

Bake for 1 hour, until the filling is bubbly and the edges are brown. Let the pecan pie cool in the pan for at least 1 hour, until solidified. Lift it out by the parchment, place it onto a cooling rack and cool completely before cutting into squares.

BASICS

I am a firm believer that homemade is best. Every single recipe in this chapter is super easy to make, and way healthier and less expensive than what you find in the stores. Once you make your own anything, you will never buy the stuff in jars again.

Cashew Cream

Makes 1 cup (240 ml)

Cashew cream is an essential ingredient in my kitchen. I use it all throughout this book, in both sweet and savory recipes. Even if you have a high-speed blender, it is a good idea to soak the cashews for at least four hours or as long as overnight, before turning them into cream. Alternatively, you can cover the nuts in boiling water and let them stand for 15 to 30 minutes. The nuts will puff up and become waterlogged, making them easier to blend. Either way, drain the soaking water, rinse the cashews and use new water to make the cream.

1 cup (146 g) raw cashews, soaked overnight, drained and rinsed

¾ cup (180 ml) water

Add the cashews and water to a blender. Blend for 1 to 2 minutes until combined. Test the texture by dipping a spoon into the mix. If it is grainy, keep blending, adding a splash or two of water, until it is the perfectly smooth texture of cream.

Store in the refrigerator for up to 3 days or in the freezer for up to 3 months. If it has thickened up, add a splash of water and mix well.

Unsalted Spreadable Butter

Makes 2½ cups (560 g)

I was inspired to make my own butter after learning Miyoko Schinner's recipe. If you don't want to make your own, I recommend Miyoko's European Style Cultured Vegan Butter or Earth Balance Organic Coconut Spread for the recipes in this book.

1 cup (240 ml) melted refined coconut oil

¾ cup (180 ml) sunflower oil

½ cup (120 ml) Cashew Cream (page 165)

2 tsp (10 ml) liquid soy lecithin

Add the oils, cashew cream and soy lecithin to a blender. Blend for 2 minutes.

Pour the butter into two containers that can be sealed airtight. Cover and place into the freezer to set. Once set, place one container in the refrigerator for everyday use.

Almond Ricotta

Makes 2 cups (456 g)

I use so much ricotta cheese in my cooking that I keep a bag of organic blanched almonds in my freezer. That way I have them on hand when I want to add some fresh ricotta to my recipes. If you don't want to make your own, I recommend Kite Hill. Even if you have a high-speed blender, it is a good idea to soak the almonds, so the ricotta comes out creamy.

1 cup (143 g) whole blanched almonds, soaked overnight, drained and rinsed

¾ cup (180 ml) filtered water, plus more, if necessary

Pinch of salt

Add the almonds, water and salt to a blender. Blend on low. As the almonds break down, turn the speed up. If the machine is not moving well, add a splash or two of water, to get it going. Blend until the ricotta is creamy and fluffy. You can test the texture by dipping a spoon into the mix and tasting it. It should be smooth and creamy. If not, add another splash of water and blend again.

Use immediately, or store in an airtight container in the refrigerator for up to 3 days.

NOTE:

If you can't find whole blanched almonds, use blanched slivered almonds. Alternatively, soak whole almonds in their skins overnight and, when they are ready, pop the skins off by pinching them between your fingers. Sometimes they go flying, but you will get the hang of it!

Grainy Mustard

Makes about 2 cups (480 ml)

You are probably saying to yourself, "I can make my own mustard?" I am here to say, yes you can! It's easier than you may have imagined, you control the ingredients, and it lasts forever in the refrigerator. Trust me, it's so good that I started giving it out as Christmas presents.

The basic recipe calls for apple cider vinegar, but change it up and try white wine vinegar, maple vinegar or sherry vinegar. And, you can sweeten the mustard by adding 1 tablespoon (15 ml) of golden maple syrup to the mix.

¼ cup (44 g) yellow mustard seeds
¼ cup (44 g) brown mustard seeds
½ cup (120 ml) apple cider vinegar
½ cup plus 2 tbsp (150 ml) water
½ tsp sea salt

Place the mustard seeds, vinegar, water and salt in a jar with a lid. Seal the lid tightly. Shake it up and let it sit for 24 hours.

Add the entire mixture to a blender. Blend until the mustard is smooth with flecks of yellow and brown. Transfer back into the jar, place in the refrigerator and use in any recipe that calls for grainy mustard.

All-Purpose Red Sauce

Makes 3½ cups (840 ml)

This sauce was one of the first things I taught myself how to make when I started cooking and it is a staple in my kitchen. I haven't bought jarred sauce since. After you make your own, you won't either. I went through a lot of iterations, and a lot of garlic, including one batch of sauce that included an entire head, but I finally landed on this formula for my go-to, all-purpose sauce.

2 tbsp (30 ml) good olive oil

2 big cloves garlic, pressed

1 (4.5-oz [127-g]) tube of tomato paste

1 tsp salt

1 (28-oz [794-g]) can crushed tomatoes

1 cup (240 ml) water

Heat a heavy bottomed pot over low heat. Add the oil. When it is shimmering, add the garlic. Sauté until fragrant, about 2 minutes.

Add the tomato paste. Use a wooden spoon to mix the tomato paste into the oil and garlic, cooking it for 3 to 4 minutes. Add the salt.

Add the can of tomatoes to the pot. Add the water to the can and swirl it around so that you get the rest of whatever is left. Pour it into the pot and stir. Bring the sauce up to a nice simmer. Cook, uncovered, for 45 minutes, stirring occasionally, until the sauce has thickened.

Use immediately, or store in sealed jars in the refrigerator for up to 1 week or in the freezer for up to 3 months.

Nut Milk

Makes 4 cups (960 ml)

Homemade nut milk is a great alternative to buying the already-made-stuff in the stores. It's easy to make and you can have plant-based milk whenever you want it. The best nuts for milk are cashews, blanched almonds and Brazil nuts. Cashews are the easiest; the milk doesn't have to be strained. Almond milk and Brazil nut milk both need to be strained, so run the milk through a fine-mesh strainer or squeeze it through a nut milk bag.

Sweeten the milk with maple syrup or dates, or flavor it with a touch of vanilla extract, ground vanilla beans and/or cinnamon, or make chocolate milk by adding cacao powder. Experiment and figure out your favorite combination. Even if you have a high-speed blender, it is a good idea to soak the nuts.

1 cup (150 g) raw nuts, soaked overnight, drained and rinsed

3 cups (720 ml) water

Add the nuts and water to a blender. Blend for 1 to 2 minutes.

If using almonds or Brazil nuts, pour the milk through a fine-mesh strainer over a bowl or squeeze the milk through a nut milk bag.

Pour the milk into a bottle and seal it tightly. Store in the refrigerator for up to 3 days or in the freezer for up to 3 months.

Almond Parmesan

Makes 1⅓ cups (150 g)

A vegan Parmesan-style topping is a non-negotiable vegan kitchen staple. A big batch lasts for what seems like forever. Use it to complement everything Italian-esque, and add it to salads or anything else that could use a cheesy topping. My secret? Super-fine, light and fluffy blanched almond flour and dried lemon zest for a little extra brightness.

Dried Lemon Zest
1 lemon

Almond Parmesan
1 cup (104 g) super-fine blanched almond flour
⅓ cup (43 g) nutritional yeast
1 tbsp (4 g) dried lemon zest
1 tsp onion powder
1 tsp salt

To make the dried lemon zest, wash the skin of a lemon really well. Zest the lemon over a piece of parchment paper. You should get about 1 tablespoon (6 g) of zest. Let the zest hang out on the counter for a few hours until it's completely dry. Crush it up between your fingers until it is a fine powder.

To make the almond Parmesan, preheat the oven to 350°F (175°C, or gas mark 4). Spread the almond flour on a half sheet pan into as thin a layer as possible.

Toast the flour until golden, 10 to 15 minutes.

When the almond flour has cooled, place it into a big mixing bowl. Add the nutritional yeast, dried lemon zest, onion powder and salt. Mix well.

Store in a sealed container in the refrigerator and use whenever you want a cheesy topping.

Seasoned Breadcrumbs

Makes about 2 cups (240 g)

My mother used to have a can of seasoned breadcrumbs in the pantry, until I started helping her in the kitchen. I insisted we make our own because I had seen an old chef make them on television once. Truly, they could not be easier to make, and it's one more basic ingredient you will never buy from the store again.

1 (20-inch [51-cm]) day-old baguette or your favorite bread

¼ packed cup (18 g) fresh parsley

¼ cup (32 g) nutritional yeast

1 tbsp (5 g) dried oregano

1 tbsp (8 g) garlic powder

1 tbsp (7 g) onion powder

1 tsp paprika

1 tsp sea salt

Preheat the oven to 350°F (175°C, or gas mark 4). Line a half sheet pan with parchment paper.

Cut the bread into 1-inch (2.5-cm) slices and place on the sheet pan. Bake for 10 minutes, flip the slices over and bake for another 5 minutes. Turn the oven off. Place the parsley on the sheet pan with the bread and let everything hang out for another 5 to 10 minutes as the oven cools down, to ensure the bread and parsley are totally dried out.

Remove the sheet pan from the oven, and let the bread and parsley cool. Add the bread slices to a food processor in small batches, and process until coarse crumbs form. When they have broken down, add the nutritional yeast, parsley, oregano, garlic powder, onion powder, paprika and salt. Pulse until the parsley is minced and the crumbs are fine.

Store in a sealed container for up to 6 months.

The Little Pie Crust

Makes 1

A good vegan pie crust recipe is essential. This one is made with melted refined coconut oil and bakes up crispy and buttery just like a good pie crust should. It's totally fuss-free and works every time. Just bring the ingredients together, roll it out, fill it and bake it. You can even make it a day or two ahead of time. Just wrap the ball of dough up in plastic wrap and store it in the refrigerator. When you are ready to use it, bring it up to room temperature and roll it out.

1 cup (125 g) all-purpose flour
1 tsp salt
1 tsp coconut sugar
⅓ cup (80 ml) melted refined coconut oil
3 tbsp (45 ml) water, room temperature

Line your counter with a few pieces of plastic wrap, wide enough for rolling out the dough.

Add the flour, salt and coconut sugar to a big mixing bowl. Mix to combine.

Add the oil and water to a measuring cup with a spout. Whisk to combine. Pour into the flour.

Mix the dough together with a small silicone spoonula or wooden spoon. It will come together quickly and easily. Lift the dough out of the bowl and use your hands to form it into a ball.

Drop the dough onto the middle of the plastic and cover with another piece of plastic wrap. As you roll out the dough, you will need to add another piece or two to completely cover the top.

Use a rolling pin, and with even pressure, roll out the dough, turning it every so often, to about 12 inches (30 cm) around and ⅛-inch (3-mm) thick. Run your palms over the crust to feel if it is evenly rolled out. If there are thicker spots, roll it again. Use as desired.

ACKNOWLEDGMENTS

Whenever I get a new cookbook, I flip to the back to read the acknowledgments. Last year, I got a book in which the author thanked Page Street Publishing for taking a chance on her. I thought to myself, maybe they would take a chance on me. They did . . . and now I get to say thank you.

To Will Kiester and Marissa Giambelluca, thank you for all of your support and making this process fun and exciting. To Meg Baskis, thank you for designing such a pretty book, and to Jenna Nelson Patton, thank you for being the copyeditor who made it better. And to everyone else at Page Street, thank you for all of your hard work. To Jill Browning, thank you for forwarding my original proposal. This is a dream come true and it would not have happened without you all.

To Alex Shytsman, thank you for turning my living room into a set, for being so collaborative and for taking the absolutely beautiful photographs. What a fun and creative week. Let's do it again!

To Aleen LaPrelle, thank you for testing every single recipe in this book, for coming into town to cook with me in person and for the hot sauce.

To everyone who has read and shared my blog, thank you for your interest over the last nine years!

To Joy Pierson, Bart Potenza, Dr. Neal Barnard, Dr. Robert Ostfeld, Rachel Atcheson, Brooklyn Borough President Eric Adams, Joey Arbagey, Hannah Kaminsky, Gena Hamshaw, Fran Costigan, Selma Miriam, Linda Soper-Kolton, Stepfanie Romine, Liz Dee and Bob Roth, thank you all for your inspiration and support.

To Alison, Andy and Sylvie, thank you for making my recipes and serving them to me, for trying everything I bring over and for enthusiastically picking up leftovers. A special thank you for the raspberries.

To my parents, Diana and Jerry, thank you for raising me to believe that I could do anything.

To my sister Debbie and my nephew Jonah, thank you for asking the best questions and for being my biggest cheerleaders.

To my son Luke, this book was your idea. Thank you for thinking I could actually do this and for being so incredibly encouraging, understanding and most of all, compassionate!

To my husband Paul, what a ride. You have my heart. Thank you for everything.

ABOUT THE AUTHOR

Lisa Dawn Angerame lives in New York City with her husband and son. A longtime vegan, she is the creator of Lisa's Project: Vegan, lisasprojectvegan.com, a blog chronicling her vegan cooking adventures. Lisa Dawn holds a certificate in Plant-Based Nutrition from eCornell and graduated from the Rouxbe Online Culinary School, rouxbe.com, as a certified Plant-Based Professional and from the Essential Vegan Desserts course. She is committed to expanding awareness about veganism by making delicious food and believes that chocolate chip cookies are the key to happiness.

INDEX